Wrap-Up (15 m

This c
point" a
priate fashion.

HomeBuilders Project (60 minutes)

This project is the unique application step in a HomeBuilders study. Before leaving a meeting, couples are encouraged to "Make a Date" to do the project for the session prior to the next meeting. Most HomeBuilders Projects contain three sections: (1) As a Couple—a brief exercise designed to get the date started, (2) Individually—a section of questions for husbands and wives to answer separately, and (3) Interact as a Couple—an opportunity for couples to share their answers with each other and to make application in their lives.

Another feature you will find in this course is a section of Parent-Child Interactions. There is a corresponding interaction for each session. These interactions provide parents an excellent opportunity to communicate with their children on the important topics covered in this course.

In addition to the above regular features, occasional activities are labeled "For Extra Impact." These are activities that generally provide a more active or visual way to make a particular point. Be mindful that people within a group have different learning styles. While most of what is presented is verbal, a visual or active exercise now and then helps engage more of the senses and appeals to people who learn best by seeing, touching, and doing.

About the Author

Bob Lepine is known to Christian radio listeners across the country as the co-host of the popular daily radio program "FamilyLife Today" with Dennis Rainey. He speaks on marriage and family at conferences and events worldwide. He is the author of the book *The Christian Husband* (Servant Publications, 1999) and a regular contributor to books and magazines.

A veteran of Christian radio, Bob oversees all radio planning and production for FamilyLife, the development of books and taped resources, and the Internet site: www.familylife.com. He received a communications degree from the University of Tulsa in 1978. Since that time, Bob has worked for a variety of Christian and mainstream radio stations in Tulsa, Phoenix, Sacramento, and San Antonio. Prior to joining FamilyLife in 1992, he hosted his own live radio talk show and held various other broadcasting positions, including news anchor, sales manager, and station general manager. Bob is a member of the board of directors for the National Religious Broadcasters.

Bob and his wife, Mary Ann, have been married since 1979. They have five children and make their home in Little Rock, Arkansas.

HomeBuilders Parenting Series™

Helping Your Children Know God

By Bob Lepine

"Unless the Lord builds the house, its builders labor in vain"
(Psalm 127:1a).

FAMILYLIFE
Bringing Timeless Principles Home
Little Rock, Arkansas

Group
Loveland, Colorado

Group's R.E.A.L. Guarantee® to you:
This Group resource incorporates our R.E.A.L. approach to ministry—one that encourages long-term retention and life transformation. It's ministry that's:

Relational
Because learner-to-learner interaction enhances learning and builds Christian friendships.

Experiential
Because what learners experience through discussion and action sticks with them up to 9 times longer than what they simply hear or read.

Applicable
Because the aim of Christian education is to equip learners to be both hearers and doers of God's Word.

Learner-based
Because learners understand and retain more when the learning process takes into consideration how they learn best.

Helping Your Children Know God
Copyright © 2004 Bob Lepine

All rights reserved. No part of this book may be reproduced in any manner whatsoever without prior written permission from the publisher, except where noted in the text and in the case of brief quotations embodied in critical articles and reviews. For information, write Permissions, Group Publishing, Inc., Dept. PD, P.O. Box 481, Loveland, CO 80539.

Visit our Web site: **www.grouppublishing.com**

Credits
FamilyLife
Editor: David Boehi

Group Publishing, Inc.
Editor: Matt Lockhart
Chief Creative Officer: Joani Schultz
Copy Editor: Janis Sampson
Art Directors: Jenette L. McEntire, Jean Bruns, and Randy Kady
Print Production Artist: Pat Miller
Cover Art Director: Jeff A. Storm
Cover Designer: Alan Furst, Inc.
Cover Photographer: Daniel Treat
Illustrator: Ken Jacobson
Production Manager: Peggy Naylor

Unless otherwise noted, Scripture taken from the HOLY BIBLE, NEW INTERNATIONAL VERSION®. Copyright © 1973, 1978, 1984 by International Bible Society. Used by permission of Zondervan Publishing House. All rights reserved.

ISBN 0-7644-2553-6
10 9 8 7 6 5 4 3 2 1   13 12 11 10 09 08 07 06 05 04

Printed in the United States of America.

HOMEBUILDERS PARENTING SERIES™

How to Let the Lord Build Your House
and not labor in vain

The HomeBuilders Parenting Series™: A small-group Bible study dedicated to making your family all that God intended.

FamilyLife is a division of Campus Crusade for Christ International, an evangelical Christian organization founded in 1951 by Bill Bright. FamilyLife was started in 1976 to help fulfill the Great Commission by strengthening marriages and families and then equipping them to go to the world with the gospel of Jesus Christ. The Weekend to Remember conference is held in most major cities throughout the United States and is one of the fastest-growing marriage conferences in America today. "FamilyLife Today," a daily radio program hosted by Dennis Rainey, is heard on hundreds of stations across the country. Information on all resources offered by FamilyLife may be obtained by contacting us at the address, telephone number, or World Wide Web site listed below.

Dennis Rainey, Executive Director
FamilyLife
P.O. Box 8220
Little Rock, AR 72221-8220
1-800-FL-TODAY
www.familylife.com

A division of Campus Crusade for Christ International
Bill Bright, Founder
Steve Douglass, President

HELPING YOUR CHILDREN KNOW GOD

About the Sessions

Each session in this study is composed of the following categories: Warm-Up, Blueprints, Wrap-Up, and HomeBuilders Project. A description of each of these categories follows:

Warm-Up (15 minutes)

The purpose of Warm-Up is to help people unwind from a busy day and get to know each other better. Typically the first point in Warm-Up is an exercise that is meant to be fun while introducing the topic of the session. The ability to share in fun with others is important in building relationships. Another component of Warm-Up is the Project Report (except in Session One), which is designed to provide accountability for the HomeBuilders Project that is to be completed by couples between sessions.

Blueprints (60 minutes)

This is the heart of the study. In this part of each session, people answer questions related to the topic of study and look to God's Word for understanding. Some of the questions are to be answered by couples, in subgroups, or in the group at large. There are notes in the margin or instructions within a question that designate these groupings.

Contents

Acknowledgments **8**

Introduction **9**

Session One: Getting to Know God **13**

Session Two: Getting to Know God Through Creation...........**25**

Session Three: Learning About God Through the Bible......**37**

Session Four: Learning About God Through
  His Attributes...**51**

Session Five: Learning About God Through Jesus Christ **65**

Session Six: Responding to God **81**

Parent-Child Interactions...**97**

Where Do You Go From Here? **111**

Our Problems, God's Answers **114**

Leader Notes **124**

Acknowledgments

My hope for this study is that many moms and dads will grow in their own understanding of our great God and will be challenged and equipped to pass that understanding on to a new generation. If this study achieves that objective, there are many people to thank. First, there are those who have helped shape my own understanding about God: Wayne Grudem, R.C. Sproul, John Piper, John MacArthur, and J.I. Packer have been some of my mentors from a distance, and I owe them a great debt. Dennis Rainey has been a mentor and friend who has sharpened my thinking about God's purposes and plan for marriage and family.

Two skillful craftsmen have made this a better, clearer tool. Dave Boehi and Matt Lockhart took my first draft and fine-tuned it. Meanwhile, many of my friends and co-workers at FamilyLife took up the slack when I was off-site reading and writing. Chief among them is Christy Bain, who handles many things on my behalf. In addition, without Mike Clower's leadership as the director of broadcasting at FamilyLife, I could not have taken the time to complete this project.

I am often convicted as I write by how poorly I execute my own counsel. I am grateful to God for his grace that covers a multitude of my sins of omission as a parent. I have no greater joy than to know that my children are walking in the truth (3 John 4), in spite of my own shortcomings as a spiritual leader. *Soli Deo Gloria!*

Introduction

Nearly all of the important jobs in our culture require intensive training. We would not think of allowing someone to practice medicine, for example, without first attending medical school and completing a residency.

But do you realize that most people receive little training in how to fulfill one of the most important responsibilities of our lives—being effective parents? When we bring a new life into the world, we burst with pride and joy...but are often ignorant of how to actually raise that child to become a mature, responsible adult.

In response to the need we see in families today, FamilyLife and Group Publishing have developed a series of small-group studies called the HomeBuilders Parenting Series. These studies focus on raising children and are written so that parents of children of all ages will benefit.

For these HomeBuilders studies, we have several goals in mind: First, *we want to encourage you in the process of child rearing*. We feel that being a mom or a dad is a high calling and an incredible privilege. We also know how easy it is to feel overwhelmed by the responsibility, especially when you have young children. Participating in a HomeBuilders group can connect you with other parents who share your struggles. The help and encouragement you receive from them will be invaluable.

Second, *we want to help you develop a practical, biblical plan for parenting*. It's so easy for parents to take parenting one day at a time. But as we've raised our children, we've learned that we need to understand biblical guidelines on parenting and then make proactive plans on how we will apply them.

Third, *we want to enhance and strengthen your teamwork as a couple*. You will learn together how to apply key biblical truths, and in the HomeBuilders Projects you will talk through how to apply them to your unique family situation. In the process, you will have the opportunity to discuss issues that you may have ignored or avoided in the past. And you'll spend time regularly in prayer, asking God for his direction and power.

Fourth, *we want to help you connect with other parents so you can encourage and help one another.* You could complete this study with just your spouse, but we strongly urge you to either form or join a group of couples studying this material. You will find that the questions in each study will help create a special environment of warmth, encouragement, and fellowship as you meet together to study how to build the type of home you desire. You will have the opportunity to talk with other parents to learn some new ideas...or to get their advice...or just to see that others are going through the same experiences. Participating in a HomeBuilders group could be one of the highlights of your life.

Finally, *we want to help you strengthen your relationship with God.* Not only does our loving Father provide biblical principles for parenting, but our relationship with him allows us to rely on his strength and wisdom. In fact, it is when we feel most power-less and inadequate as parents that he is most real to us. God loves to help the helpless parent.

The Bible: Blueprints for Building Your Family

You will notice as you proceed through this study that the Bible is used frequently as the final authority on issues of life, marriage, and parenting. Although written thousands of years ago, this Book still speaks clearly and powerfully about the struggles we face in our families. The Bible is God's Word—his blueprint for building a God-honoring home and for dealing with the practical issues of living.

We encourage you to have a Bible with you for each session. For this series we use the New International Version as our primary reference. Another excellent translation is the New American Standard Bible.

A Special Word to Single Parents

Although the primary audience for this study is married couples, we recognize that single parents will benefit greatly from the experience. If you are a single parent, you will find that some of the language and material does not apply directly to you. But most of what you will find in this study is timeless wisdom taken directly from Scripture and can help you develop a solid, workable plan for your family. We hope you will be flexible and adapt the material to your specific situation.

If possible, you might want to attend the group sessions with another single parent. This will allow you to encourage each other and hold each other accountable to complete the HomeBuilders Projects.

Ground Rules

Each group is designed to be enjoyable and informative— and non-threatening. Three simple ground rules will help ensure that everyone feels comfortable and gets the most out of the experience.

1. Don't share anything that would embarrass your spouse or violate the trust of your children.

2. You may pass on any question you don't want to answer.

3. If possible, plan to complete the HomeBuilders Project as a couple between group sessions.

INTRODUCTION

A Few Quick Notes About Leading a HomeBuilders Group

1. Leading a group is much easier than you may think! A group leader in a HomeBuilders session is really a "facilitator." As a facilitator, your goal is simply to guide the group through the discussion questions. You don't need to teach the material—in fact, we don't want you to! The special dynamic of a HomeBuilders group is that couples teach themselves.

2. This material is designed to be used in a home study, but it also can be adapted for use in a Sunday school environment. (See pages 125-126—"In a Sunday school class"—for more information about this option.)

3. We have included a section of Leader Notes in the back of this book. Be sure to read through these notes before leading a session; they will help you prepare.

4. For more material on leading a HomeBuilders group, get a copy of the *HomeBuilders Leader Guide* by Drew and Kit Coons. This book is an excellent resource that provides helpful guidelines on how to start a study, how to keep discussion moving, and much more.

Session One

Getting to Know God

Our primary assignment as parents is to show our children how they can know God.

W A R M • U P   15 MINUTES

Introductions

Take a couple of minutes to introduce yourself to someone in the group you don't know very well (man to man, woman to woman). Find out each other's names, names and ages of each other's children, and one other fact. After everyone has had an opportunity to visit, take turns introducing each other to the group. Then discuss these questions:

- What do you find both exciting and fun or intimidating and hard about getting to know someone?
- In what ways is introducing someone to others like or unlike introducing a child to God?

Getting Connected

Pass your books around the room, and have everyone write in their names, phone numbers, and e-mail addresses.

_____
NAME, PHONE, AND E-MAIL

_____
NAME, PHONE, AND E-MAIL

_____
NAME, PHONE, AND E-MAIL

_____
NAME, PHONE, AND E-MAIL

_____
NAME, PHONE, AND E-MAIL

_____
NAME, PHONE, AND E-MAIL

BLUEPRINTS   60 MINUTES

> If you have a large group, form smaller groups of about six people to answer the Blueprints questions. Unless otherwise noted, answer the questions in your subgroup. Before moving on to the Wrap-Up section, have subgroups report to the whole group the highlights from their discussions.

First Impressions

1. What is one perception—accurate or inaccurate—you remember having about God as a young child?

2. About how old were you when you first recall hearing or thinking about God? Who first told you about God? How accurate was their information?

Influences

3. In addition to what you heard about God as a child, which of the following have had a significant impact on your view of God? Take a minute to rank these in order of their influence on you, from 1 (the most) to 6 (the least). Then share with the group what you ranked as number 1 and why.

__ family

__ church

__ school

__ media (books, magazines, music, movies, television, Internet)

__ the Bible

__ opinions of others (non-family: peers, friends, neighbors, co-workers)

__ other: _____

Answer question 4 with your spouse. After answering, you may want to share an appropriate insight or discovery with the group.

4. How would you rank the items in question 3 for each of your children?

5. Read Deuteronomy 6:5-9 and Psalm 78:1-8. What do you take from these passages about *what* and *how* we ought to teach our children? What can happen if we fail to teach them about God and his ways?

HomeBuilders Principle:
God wants all of us—including our children—to know him.

Making an Introduction

Pretend that you have been asked to introduce a guest speaker for a special event. The speaker is a well-respected author and an expert on human behavior, but this person is someone you don't know anything about. You've been told that the introduction should take at least three minutes and should help the audience feel as if they really know the person when you're finished.

6. Prior to being able to make a proper introduction, what are some of the basics you need to know? As a group, come up with a list of at least five things you would like to know about the person before you made an introduction.

7. Where would you go for information? What would be your best sources?

8. How would you change your introduction if you were speaking to kindergartners? to preteens? to young adults?

9. What would be different between introducing someone you *know* versus introducing someone you only *know things about*?

SESSION ONE • GETTING TO KNOW GOD

17

10. From your discussion of the preceding questions, which elements of making an introduction do you think should also be applied to the process of introducing your children to God? Explain.

Meeting Jesus

11. With each couple taking at least one of the following questions, read John 1:35-49 and discuss your question. Then take turns reporting your answers to the group.

- What do you find typical, interesting, or unique about the introductions made in this passage?

- What process do the people in this passage go through to move from knowing about Jesus to becoming his followers?

- What do the people making the introductions (John, Andrew, and Philip) have in common?

- In comparison to the reactions of Andrew and Nathanael, what was your reaction when you were first introduced to Jesus?

12. How would you classify your relationship with God—would you say you know him or know about him? Explain.

> Answer question 12 with your spouse. After answering, you may want to share an appropriate insight or discovery with the group.

If you have never moved from being someone who knows about God to actually knowing God for yourself, we invite you to read "Our Problems, God's Answers," beginning on page 114. This article explains how to have a personal relationship with God.

> **HomeBuilders Principle:**
> *The most important requirement for introducing others to God is for you to know him yourself.*

WRAP • UP   15 MINUTES

Top Ten List

To conclude this first session, as a group discuss the following:

- What do you think are the primary

> After completing the Wrap-Up activity, close this session in prayer. Before leaving, couples are encouraged to "Make a Date" to do this session's HomeBuilders Project.

things about God that children need to understand? Create a top ten list.

1.	6.
2.	7.
3.	8.
4.	9.
5.	10.

After the group has compiled a list, answer this question with your spouse:

- How well would you say your children understand these things?

Make a Date

Make a date with your spouse to complete the
HomeBuilders Project for this session. Your leader
will ask at the next session for you to share one thing
from this experience.

DATE

TIME

LOCATION

HOMEBUILDERS PROJECT 6 0 M I N U T E S

As a Couple [10 minutes]

Kickoff this project by talking about memorable things your children have said to you about God or asked God in prayer.

- What do these things reveal about what your children know—or don't know—about God?

Individually [20 minutes]

1. Read through the questions from the group session. What is one thing from this session that you want to apply in your life?

2. Think about what your parents taught you about God when you were growing up.

• What did they do that you want to duplicate with your children?

• What do you wish they had done that they didn't do?

• What do you wish they hadn't done that they did?

3. How would you evaluate how much your children know about God? Put your child's initials next to the category that you feel best fits.

No Knowledge	Very Basic	Some Details	Better Than Average	Advanced
1	2	3	4	5

4. Looking back at the list under question 3 in the group session (p. 15), which of these do you see as positive sources of information? negative?

5. What can or should be done to counter the sources of incorrect information about God that your children face?

6. In order to be best able to help your children know God, what's something you can do to strengthen your relationship with God?

Interact as a Couple [30 minutes]

1. Share your answers from the individual section. As you discuss your responses, be open, kind, and understanding. Make an effort to listen to each other without interrupting.

2. Discuss how you can encourage and help keep each other accountable for the things you identified that can help you grow in your personal relationships with God.

3. Revisit the top ten list from the session's Wrap-Up (p. 20). For each child, identify one item from the list that you agree is something that he or she needs to better understand about God. Write down ideas of how you can help your children grow in their understanding of these items.

4. Close in prayer. Pray that your children will know God and for wisdom as you seek to help them know God.

Be sure to check out the related Parent-Child Interaction on page 97.

Session Two

Getting to Know God Through Creation

Our children can learn about God from his creation.

WARM·UP 15 MINUTES

Back to Nature

Choose one of the following questions to answer, and share with the group.

- What outdoor activities do you enjoy doing as a family?
- What is one thing you have learned about your spouse by spending time with him or her in the great outdoors that you didn't know when you were first married? (Be nice!)
- When have you seen or experienced evidence of God in nature?

For Extra Impact

Nature Walk:

Use this activity for a more active, hands-on Warm-Up.

As a group, take a five-minute walk outside. On your walk, look for evidence of God in creation. Then come back in and discuss this question:

- What did you discover that testifies to the existence of the Creator?

Project Report

Share one thing you learned from last session's HomeBuilders Project.

BLUEPRINTS — 60 MINUTES

The Invisible God

A Wilderness Mystery

Imagine you're hiking in the woods in the middle of August, and you see some smoke rising above the treetops up ahead. You know that the park where you are hiking has temporarily banned all campfires because the underbrush is dangerously dry, so you go to investigate. When you come to a clearing, you find a smoldering campfire. By the fire pit are empty soup cans, empty beer cans, and hot dog remains. Up ahead, you find tire tracks in a muddy spot by an old dirt road.

If you have a large group, form smaller groups of about six people to answer the Blueprints questions. Unless otherwise noted, answer the questions in your subgroup. Before moving to the Wrap-Up section, have subgroups report to the whole group the highlights from their discussions.

1. Based on the evidence, what conclusions could you draw? What are some things you can't know for sure?

2. If you were able to find fingerprints on the cans, what additional conclusions could you reach?

3. Read John 1:18 and Colossians 1:15. How does our "wilderness mystery" compare to our trying to learn about the one described in Colossians 1:15 as

SESSION TWO • GETTING TO KNOW GOD THROUGH CREATION   **27** the "invisible God"? How can we learn about a person we can't see in the flesh?

4. What are ways that God makes himself known? Where can we find "evidence" that tells us about God?

God's Character on Display

Often we can learn about someone's personality or character by examining something that person has created.

5. Consider these items:

• the Great Pyramids

• the Eiffel Tower

• an ice-cream cone

If you didn't know anything about the people who designed or created these items, what conclusions might you draw about the creators based on the evidence—the things they created? Why?

6. Now consider some of the things God has created:

- thousands of species of butterflies
- the Grand Canyon
- an infinite universe of stars and planets
- the human eye

If you knew nothing about God other than that he has created the things listed, what conclusions might you draw about him?

7. With each couple taking one or more of the following passages, read your verses with your spouse, and discuss what we can learn about God and his character from creation. Then report to the group a summary of your verses and insights.

- Psalm 8:3-4
- Psalm 19:1-2
- Psalm 57:9-10
- Psalm 103:11-12
- Jeremiah 32:17
- Romans 1:18-20

8. What in God's creation awes or inspires you? What in nature fascinates your children? How can

SESSION TWO • GETTING TO KNOW GOD THROUGH CREATION

you use this fascination to teach your children about God?

> **HomeBuilders Principle:**
> *Even though we cannot physically see God, one way God has revealed himself to us is through his creation.*

The God of Right and Wrong

9. When it comes to knowing right and wrong, do you think that each person is born with a conscience, or do you think that each person is born with a "clean slate"? Explain.

10. There are certain things that virtually all cultures in every period of history have accepted as wrong. What are some of these things? What do you think this reveals about God?

11. Read Romans 2:14-15 and 2 Corinthians 1:12.

Where does our conscience come from, and what does it do for us?

12. How have you observed conscience at work in your children? Read Psalm 51:1-2, 10-12. What do these verses convey that you can teach your children to do when they have done something wrong?

> Answer question 12 with your spouse. After answering, you may want to share an appropriate insight or discovery with the group.

> **HomeBuilders Principle:**
> *Our innate sense of right and wrong bears witness to both the existence and character of God.*

W R A P • U P   15   MINUTES

Seeing God

As parents, we should take advantage of creation to teach our children about God—especially during

After completing the Wrap-Up activity, close this session in prayer. Before leaving, couples are encouraged to "Make a Date" to do this session's HomeBuilders Project.

their early years when they are so curious and teachable. All that's needed is a bit of creativity and the willingness to go out and see what you can learn.

Imagine you were spending time with your children in the following locations:

- at the beach
- out in the country, looking up at the stars on a clear night
- in a flower garden
- in a jet, looking out the window at thirty thousand feet
- at a local zoo or aquarium
- on a mountaintop

What different things could you point to at each location to help your children understand more about God?

With your spouse, think of a place nearby where you could take your children on an outing to experience God in nature.

Make a Date

Make a date with your spouse to complete this session's HomeBuilders Project. Your leader will ask at the next session for you to share one thing from this experience.

_____
DATE

_____
TIME

_____
LOCATION

HOMEBUILDERS PROJECT   6 0   M I N U T E S

As a Couple [10 minutes]

Start your date by discussing these questions:

- What's the most powerful force of nature you've ever witnessed? In what way, if any, did this experience cause you to think about God?

- When is a time from childhood when you "got away" with something—only then to have your conscience get the better of you, prompting you to confess?

Individually [20 minutes]

1. What is one way you were challenged by this session?

2. Read Psalm 19:1-6. How does God use the concept of "the heavens" in this passage to communicate to us about him?

3. Where—physically—do you tend to feel closest to or most aware of God? Why do you think this is?

4. What are some things you have learned about God through nature?

5. Do you think insights about God as revealed by nature are easier for adults or children to perceive? Explain.

6. What are things you can do to encourage your children to "see God" in the world around them?

7. How can the conscience be used as a tool to instruct your children about God?

Interact as a Couple [30 minutes]

1. Share your answers from the individual time.

2. Identify at least one thing on which you agree that you want to begin doing with your children that will help them get to know God better.

3. Take a few minutes to plan an outing in which you can accomplish this goal. (One idea would be to complete the Parent-Child Interaction for this session on page 99.)

Date:

Time:

Place:

4. Close in prayer, with each of you completing the following sentence: "Dear God, my prayer for our children is…"

Session Three

Learning About God Through the Bible

God reveals himself through Scripture in a variety of ways.

WARM·UP   15 MINUTES

Who's Your Superhero?

Form two groups (one men's group and one women's group). Have one group discuss ways the characters listed in the chart on the next page are like God and the other group talk about how they are unlike God. After a few minutes, each group should report on its discussion. Then answer the questions that follow the chart.

SESSION THREE • LEARNING ABOUT GOD THROUGH THE BIBLE

	Like God	Unlike God
Greek and Roman gods and goddesses		
Superheroes from movies, TV, or comic books		
Actors who have portrayed God or Jesus in movies and on TV		

- What are some beliefs about God that seem to be widely held (by adults or children), but which aren't necessarily supported by Scripture?

- What would you say are the primary sources of information about God for most people? for your children?

Project Report

Share one thing you learned from last session's HomeBuilders Project.

BLUEPRINTS **60 MINUTES**

As we saw in our last session, God has made himself known to all people through creation and by giving us a basic understanding of right and wrong. However, in order for us to really know God, we need to understand God as revealed to us in the Bible.

In this session, our focus will be on the Bible as a tool for knowing God. Then in the next session, we'll delve further into knowing God through the Scriptures by specifically focusing on some of God's attributes as found in the Bible.

If you have a large group, form smaller groups of about six people to answer the Blueprints questions. Unless otherwise noted, answer the questions in your sub-group. Before moving on to the Wrap-Up section, have subgroups report to the whole group the highlights from their discussions.

The Right Source

1. What do the following verses tell us about the Bible?
• Psalm 19:7-11

• Psalm 119:105

SESSION THREE • LEARNING ABOUT GOD THROUGH THE BIBLE **39**

• 2 Timothy 3:16

• Hebrews 4:12

2. What makes the things written in the Bible about God different from other books about God? Why is this important as we seek to help our children know God?

3. Read 2 Timothy 3:14-15. What does this passage tell us about the ability of even a young child to know "the holy Scriptures"? From your experience, what are some Bible truths that preschool age children (two to five) are able to understand?

4. The Bible is God's story, but it communicates about God in a number of different ways. With each couple taking at least one of the types of communication in the following chart, discuss the importance of this type of writing, and, in general, what kind of things or information about God can be learned from it. Then report your insights to the group.

Types of communication about God in the Bible	What this style of writing communicates to us about God
Personal letters (for example, Paul's letters to the Romans and Philippians)	
Eyewitness testimony (the Gospels)	
Poetry/Wisdom (for example, Psalms and Proverbs)	
History (for example, in the Old Testament, Judges and 1 and 2 Kings; in the New Testament, Acts)	
Prophesy (for example, in the Old Testament, Isaiah and Daniel; in the New Testament, Revelation)	
Law (the Pentateuch—the first five books of the Bible)	

HomeBuilders Principle:
God wants us to know him and has revealed himself to us in the Bible.

SESSION THREE • LEARNING ABOUT GOD THROUGH THE BIBLE

How the Bible Helps Us Know God

5. Based on what you know from the Bible, what are some basic things you believe about God? As a group, come up with a list of fifteen to twenty things.

To help your children learn more about God from the Bible, a logical place to start is to examine passages in which God talks about himself.

6. What does God say about himself in the following verses?
• Isaiah 46:9-11

• Jeremiah 31:3

• Jeremiah 32:27

• Revelation 1:8

7. What places, occasions, or settings do you think might be conducive to teaching your children about God, using Scriptures like those in question 6?

Another way to learn about God is to study the lives of biblical characters and how they learned about God through their experiences.

8. Read Psalm 32. How does David describe God? How did this knowledge of God benefit David? In what ways can David's understanding of God benefit our children and us?

A third way God reveals himself is through the stories we read in the Old and New Testaments. These narratives tell us about God's character and about how different people, including children, responded to him. And since children tend to love stories, Bible stories provide us with a great opportunity to make God's Word come alive in the minds of our children.

SESSION THREE • LEARNING ABOUT GOD THROUGH THE BIBLE

9. Read the story of the fiery furnace in Daniel 3:8-30 and the story of the prodigal son in Luke 15:11-32, and discuss these questions:

• What do we learn about God in these stories?

• What do we learn about how we should respond to God?

• What are ways you can make stories like these come alive for a preschool age child? elementary age child? teenager?

Answer question 10 with your spouse. After answering, you may want to share an appropriate insight or discovery with the group.

10. How would you rate how you've been doing to help your children know God through the Bible? What's one thing you would like to do that would help you in this area?

HomeBuilders Principle:
A key question we should teach our children to ask themselves every time they read something in the Bible is "What does this passage teach me about God?"

W R A P • U P   15 MINUTES

Brainstorm

Brainstorm a list of ways you could use the Bible with your children to help them get to know God better. Record your ideas in the space below.

With your spouse, review the list and select one idea to use between now and the next meeting.

Make a Date

Make a date with your spouse to complete the HomeBuilders Project for this session. Your leader will ask at the next session for you to share one thing from this experience.

DATE

TIME

LOCATION

HOMEBUILDERS PROJECT   6 0   M I N U T E S

As a Couple [10 minutes]

What's your favorite Bible…

- book?

- story?

- character?

- verse?

Individually [20 minutes]

1. What's one insight or concept from this session that you want to apply?

2. Read Psalm 119:105. How has the Bible been a lamp or light to you?

3. How has the Bible been a light or lamp in the lives of your children?

4. How would you evaluate your own study of the Bible? What could make it better?

5. Where are your children currently learning about God? How is the Bible used in these places?

6. What are specific ways that the Bible has helped you grow in your understanding of God?

7. What's one thing you would like to see done in your home on a regular basis to help your family get to know God better through the Bible?

Interact as a Couple [30 minutes]

1. Share your answers from the individual section.

2. For each of your children, write down one thing that you'll commit to doing over the next week, using the Bible to help your children know God better.

3. Do your children have Bibles of their own? If not, plan a family outing to a local Christian bookstore to do some Bible shopping. Find a translation that can be easily understood by your child.

4. Close in prayer.

Be sure to check out the related Parent-Child Interaction on page 101.

| Session Four |

Learning About God Through His Attributes

Knowing the attributes of God can help give your children a vision of the true God.

W A R M • U P   15 MINUTES

Descriptions

From the list of names, select one or two people, and jot down a few words you feel best describe the people you chose. Report your selections and descriptions with the group, then discuss the questions that follow the list.

Albert Einstein	Tom Hanks	Billy Graham
Harriet Tubman	Tiger Woods	Queen Esther
Serena Williams	Jackie Chan	Mother Teresa
Oprah Winfrey	Helen Keller	Hudson Taylor
Martha Stewart	Apostle Paul	Jennifer Lopez
Martin Luther King		

SESSION FOUR • LEARNING ABOUT GOD THROUGH HIS ATTRIBUTES 51

- What are three or four words you would use to describe God?

- If you asked your children to describe God, what words do you think they would use and why?

Project Report

Share one thing you learned from last session's HomeBuilders Project.

BLUEPRINTS 60 MINUTES

If you have a large group, form smaller groups of about six people to answer the Blueprints questions. Unless otherwise noted, answer the questions in your subgroup. Before moving on to the Wrap-Up section, have subgroups report to the whole group the highlights from their discussions.

As we get to know someone, we learn about his or her attributes. An attribute is an aspect of a person's character that shapes who the person is and helps us know the person. In the same way, we can improve our knowledge of God by discovering his attributes. The more we learn about who God is, the more we come to know him. And as we come to know God better, we're better able to serve and worship him.

Names of God

In ancient Israel, as people began to learn more about God, they would often declare a new name for him based on what they had learned. These different names can give us insight into who God is.

1. How did you decide on the names of your children? Do their names honor any individuals or carry a particular meaning?

2. Following are verses with some of the descriptive names ascribed to God in the Old Testament. What do these names teach us about God's character?

• Genesis 14:22

• Genesis 17:1

• Genesis 22:14

• Judges 6:24

SESSION FOUR • LEARNING ABOUT GOD THROUGH HIS ATTRIBUTES   **53**

• Isaiah 9:6

3. One common name for God found throughout the Old Testament is *Jehovah*, or *Yahweh*. The name God gives himself, "I AM WHO I AM" (Exodus 3:14) is the name we translate as *Jehovah,* or *Yahweh.* Read Exodus 3:13-15. What are some of the things we read about in this passage that make this name special? What does this name tell you about God's nature?

4. Practically, how can the names of God be used to help your children better understand the character and nature of God?

HomeBuilders Principle:
Knowing the names of God found in the Bible is an important way our children can come to know and understand more about who God is.

Lamb, Lion, Shepherd

One way the Bible helps us understand the character of God is through the titles given to him and to Jesus. These descriptions can help us—and our children—better comprehend God.

5. As a couple, select one or two of the following verses. For the verse or verses you have selected, answer these questions: What does this verse teach us about Jesus? What meaning does this verse have for us as followers of Christ? What is a creative way you could teach the truth of this verse to your children? Then report your insights to the group.

• John 1:29

• John 8:12

• John 10:11

• John 15:1

• Revelation 5:5

6. The Bible also uses a number of metaphors to help us understand things about God and his relationship to us. With each couple taking at least one of the following passages, look up your verses and complete the following statement for each: Because the Lord is…, those who follow him can…

(Example: Proverbs 18:10 tells us, "The name of the Lord is a strong tower." Therefore, because the Lord is a strong tower those who follow him can live in safety and security, knowing that he protects us.)

- Exodus 15:2-3
- 2 Samuel 22:2-3
- Psalm 23:1-3
- Psalm 27:1
- Psalm 28:7
- Isaiah 33:22

7. Think about the different descriptions and titles for God that we've been discussing. What are some real life situations that your children face in which knowing these attributes of God could provide strength and encouragement? Be specific.

The Bread of Life

With a bit of planning, you can make it interesting for your children to learn about God's attributes. For example, the following three questions can help make the concept of Christ as the "bread of life" come alive.

8. When was the hungriest you've ever been in your lifetime?

9. What would be the difference how a piece of bread tastes that you ate now compared to eating that same piece of bread after going twenty-four hours without food? Why the difference?

For Extra Impact:
For question 9, give everyone a piece of bread to eat.

10. Read John 6:35. What do you think Jesus meant when he said, "I am the bread of life. He who comes to me will never go hungry"?

SESSION FOUR • LEARNING ABOUT GOD THROUGH HIS ATTRIBUTES

11. Now look at Deuteronomy 8:3. What additional insight does this verse bring to the image of the bread of life?

Answer question 12 with your spouse. After answering, you may want to share an appropriate insight or discovery with the group.

12. From all the names, titles, and descriptions of God that have been discussed in this session, what is one that you would like to share with your children? Discuss how you could teach or present this aspect of God to your children in an interesting or creative way.

WRAP•UP   15 MINUTES

Our Unique God

With your spouse, select seven attributes of God that you would like to focus on over the next week with your children. Assign each of these to one day of the week (for example, Monday: faithfulness, Tuesday: lovingkindness, and so on). Then as a group, discuss easy, everyday ways in which attributes of God can be communicated with your children.

Make a Date

Make a date with your spouse to complete the HomeBuilders Project for this session. Your leader will ask at the next session for you to share one thing from this experience.

_____
DATE

_____
TIME

_____
LOCATION

Parting Thought

Some of the attributes of God can be especially challenging to explain to our children. One example is the fact that God is eternal and infinite. God has no beginning and no ending. When I try to imagine infinity, my head starts to hurt!

The bottom line is that, although God reveals himself to us in many ways, ultimately there are things we cannot understand about God. These are the things

SESSION FOUR • LEARNING ABOUT GOD THROUGH HIS ATTRIBUTES   **59** that are, as Job said, "too wonderful" for us—and our children—to know (Job 42:3).

Author's note: *FamilyLife has designed a collection of twelve Christmas tree ornaments, called Adorenaments, designed to teach children different names and titles for Jesus. The ornaments include a small booklet to help you teach your children about what the various names for Jesus mean. In addition, FamilyLife has produced a CD called* Adore Him, *in which the verses for the names of Jesus have been put to music for families to learn together. For more information about either resource, call FamilyLife at 1-800-FL-TODAY (1-800-358-6329) or look online at www.familylife.com.*

HOMEBUILDERS PROJECT   6 0   M I N U T E S

As a Couple [10 minutes]

Think of at least one praiseworthy attribute that you see and admire in your spouse and take turns telling each other what this is. Then together identify at least one God-honoring trait or quality that you see in each of your children.

Individually [20 minutes]

1. What's one way that you were challenged by this session?

2. Review the questions you discussed in the group session. What is an attribute of God that is especially impressive or meaningful to you and why?

3. Look at the following list of some of God's attributes and names and then answer the questions that follow.

Names of God

Elohim—strong one; the most used Hebrew word for God (Genesis 1:1)

El Elyon—God most high (Psalm 57:2)

El Roi—God who sees (Genesis 16:13)

El Shaddai—God almighty (Job 8:5)

Adonai—Lord (Deuteronomy 9:26)

Yahweh or Jehovah—I am what I have always been (Exodus 6:3)

Jehovah Jireh—the Lord will provide (Genesis 22:14)

Jehovah Rapha—the Lord my healer, or who heals (Hosea 6:1)

Jehovah Nissi—the Lord my banner (Exodus 17:15)

Jehovah Mekoddishkem—the Lord who satisfies (Psalm 36:8)

Jehovah Shalom—the Lord my peace (Judges 6:24)

Jehovah Sabaoth—the Lord of hosts (Psalm 46:7)

Jehovah Rohi—the Lord my shepherd (Psalm 23:1)

Jehovah Tsidkenu—the Lord my righteousness (Jeremiah 23:6)
Jehovah Shammah—the Lord who is there (Hebrews 13:5)

Attributes of God

Holy (Revelation 4:8)
Lofty, or high and lifted up (Isaiah 6:1)
Omniscient (1 John 3:20)
Omnipresent (Psalm 139:7-12)
Omnipotent (Job 42:2)
Pure (2 Samuel 22:27)
Righteous (Deuteronomy 32:4)
Loving (1 John 4:8)
Forgiving (Numbers 14:18)
Just (Psalm 89:14)
Full of grace (John 1:14)
Merciful (Psalm 86:15)
Longsuffering (Exodus 34:6)
Sovereign (1 Timothy 6:15)

- What are some examples of God's attributes that we can share (demonstrate or reflect in our lives)?

- What are some attributes that are wholly unique to God?

• What is one element of God's character that you particularly need to experience in your life right now? (For example, *Jehovah-Rapha* means "God is our healer." Are you in the midst of a struggle with sickness or injury? Is there a relationship in your life that needs God's healing touch?)

• Now do the same for your children. What circumstances are they facing for which they need to experience the power of one or more of God's attributes?

• What is one attribute of God that you would most like to better display to your family? Why?

Interact as a Couple [30 minutes]

1. Share your answers from the individual section.

2. For each of your children, write down one attribute of God that would be helpful for him or her to learn and why. Make a plan for how you can begin to teach your children about these attributes.

3. Close in prayer. Thank God for his attributes, and seek his help in teaching these to your children.

Be sure to check out the related Parent-Child Interaction on page 103.

Session Five

Learning About God Through Jesus Christ

To really know God, you and your children must know Jesus Christ.

WARM·UP   15 MINUTES

Just Like You

Select one or two of the following five questions to respond to.

- What are the most apparent ways in which your children take after you or your spouse?
- Who do your friends generally say your children take after and why?
- What kind of things have you found that you can learn about a child's parents by observing their child?

- What's one thing you hope someone could know or determine about you through knowing your children?
- What's one way that knowing Jesus helps you better understand and know God?

Project Report

Share one thing you learned from last session's HomeBuilders Project.

BLUEPRINTS   60 MINUTES

God is revealed to us in many ways. Perhaps the most extraordinary revelation can be seen in God's Living Word—Jesus Christ. In Jesus we are able to see God.

Fully God and Fully Human

1. What do the following verses tell us about Jesus Christ?
- John 1:1-5, 14

- John 14:5-11

- Colossians 1:13-20

If you have a large group, form smaller groups of about six people to answer the Blueprints questions. Unless otherwise noted, answer the questions in your sub-group. Before moving into the Wrap-Up section, have subgroups report to the whole group the highlights from their discussions.

2. How did Jesus demonstrate that he possessed God's power (fully God) while here on earth? In what ways did Jesus show himself to be fully human?

Fully God	Fully human

SESSION FIVE • LEARNING ABOUT GOD THROUGH JESUS CHRIST   **67**

Revealing God's Character

Different stories about Christ reveal different aspects of God's character. These stories can be used by you to teach your children about God by drawing parallels between the character of Jesus and the character of God.

3. What insights do the following passages give us into the character of Jesus?
• Mark 2:13-17

• Mark 6:30-37

• John 4:1-9

4. What insights do these passages give us into the character of God?
• Exodus 34:5-7a

• Psalm 51:1

• Psalm 116:5

What comparisons do you see between the examples of the compassion of God and the compassion of Jesus?

5. What are a couple of practical ways children can show Christlike compassion toward others? Who would you like to see your children learn to show more compassion toward? How can the example of Christ assist us in teaching compassion to our children?

6. Read John 2:13-16. Why do you think Jesus was so angered by what was going on at the Temple?

7. While it's true that God is loving, merciful, and compassionate, God also can become angry. What do Exodus 15:7 and Joshua 23:16 tell us about God's anger?

8. What's something that makes you angry? that makes your children angry?

9. How could you use the verses from question 7 to teach your children about the difference between our anger and God's anger?

10. Read Luke 23:32-43. What does how Jesus responds to others while he is on the cross reveal about his character? the character of God?

11. Through Christ's sacrificial death on the cross, God offers us forgiveness of our sins. Colossians 3:13 tells us, "Bear with each other and forgive whatever grievances you may have against one another. Forgive as the Lord forgave you." How can knowing Jesus help us and our children be able to forgive others? In what situations do your children need to learn to forgive others just as God forgives us?

12. With your spouse, discuss the following:
• On an individual basis for each of your children, how would you evaluate your children's understanding of Jesus?

• What is one way you can help and encourage your children to grow in their understanding and relationship with God through Jesus?

WRAP • UP   15 MINUTES

Following Jesus

Jesus had another reason for living on earth. Not only did Jesus show us God's character, but he also offered his perfect life as a sacrifice for our sins so that we can be reconciled to God.

- What are some of the obstacles that can keep children from knowing God and following Jesus?

- How do our attitudes and actions about our relationship with God affect our children?

- What can we do as parents to remove obstacles that might be keeping our children from following Jesus?

For Extra Impact

Faith Stories:

If you have a large group, break into smaller groups of four to six for this activity.

Part of being a Christ-follower is telling others the good news of what God has done for you! In your group, take turns telling your faith story by responding to these questions:

- When do you recall first hearing and understanding that God wanted to have a personal relationship with you?
- How have you responded to God's invitation to a relationship with him through Jesus?

Make a Date

Make a date with your spouse to complete the HomeBuilders Project for this session. Your leader will ask at the next session for you to share one thing from this experience.

DATE

TIME

LOCATION

Parting Thought

If you have unresolved questions about what it means to know God through Jesus, you are encouraged to read the article "Our Problems, God's Answers" (p. 114).

As stated in the first session, our priority assignment as parents is to introduce our children to God. We can pray for them, teach them about God, and be living examples of what knowing God looks like. But we can't establish a relationship with God on their behalf. Ultimately, our children will either choose to respond to God's grace, or they will live in rebellion and independence from God.

A relationship with Jesus begins when we turn from our self-centeredness, come to Christ for forgiveness, and follow him. As parents, we want to continue to point our children in this direction throughout their lives.

Author's note: *We should always be thrilled when a child at any age expresses an interest in knowing or following God. We should encourage our children to pray and read the Bible (or have us read it to them). But we should not assume that all children who "ask Jesus into their hearts" at a young age have necessarily become committed followers of Jesus. For more help on understanding this issue, you may want to listen to the FamilyLife tape series* How Children Come to Faith in Christ. *You can order the tapes by calling FamilyLife at 1-800-FL-TODAY (1-800-358-6329) or by looking online at www.familylife.com.*

HOMEBUILDERS PROJECT   60 MINUTES

As a Couple [10 minutes]

Start this project by looking through baby albums—your children's albums as well as your own. (If you are out on a date for this project, do this part later at home.) As you look through these books, discuss the following:

- What similarities do you see between your children and you? between you and your parents?
- In addition to physical appearance, in what other ways (mentally, spiritually, emotionally) are your children like you and you like your parents?

Individually [20 minutes]

1. What insight or concept from this session do you most need to apply?

2. What's your favorite story about Christ and why?

3. When you think of Jesus Christ, what impresses you the most?

4. When did you first understand what it means to know God personally? Describe how you heard the gospel and responded to it.

5. How would you rate what your children know and understand about the life of Christ?

6. What's one practical way you can help your children learn more about Jesus?

7. Read 1 Corinthians 15:1-3. How well would you say that your children understand the essence of the gospel—"that Christ died for our sins"?

Interact as a Couple [30 minutes]

1. Share your answers from the individual time.

2. For your children to establish a personal relationship with God, they must understand their standing before God and make a heart commitment to respond to God in repentance and faith. For each of your children, discuss how well you think they understand the following:

• Each of us is naturally selfish and sinful, and therefore we are separated from God (Isaiah 53:6; Romans 3:10-12, 23).

• It is impossible for us to please God or earn salvation by our own efforts (Proverbs 14:12).

• Jesus Christ died on the cross to pay the penalty for our sins and make it possible for us to enjoy a relationship with God (John 14:6; Romans 5:8).

• To enjoy eternal life and establish a relationship with God, each of us must respond to God by turning from sin, receiving the gift of salvation God offers through Christ, and making Christ the Lord of our life (John 1:12; 3:16; 5:24; Ephesians 2:4-9).

3. There are many ways to emphasize the gospel to your children on a regular basis. For example, you can tell them your own faith story of how you became a Christ-follower. You can share Scriptures with them explaining their spiritual state and their need for Christ. When you discipline them for wrong choices, you can gently but firmly explain that this behavior is a natural outgrowth of their sinful hearts.

Talk for a few minutes about how you could do a better job of telling your children about Christ, his sacrifice on the cross, and their need for his gift of salvation. (Be sure to check out the related Parent-Child Interaction on page 104. This project is designed to help you help your children learn more about their need for Christ.)

4. Pray for your children to grow in their knowledge of and relationship with Jesus Christ.

Author's note: *The gospel answers the question: "How is it possible for the relationship between God and man, which was broken by our sin, to be restored?" We can answer that question in one of two ways—we can seek to do something to somehow mend the relationship, or we can put our confidence and trust in what Christ has done on our behalf to mend the relationship.*

As you communicate the good news of the gospel to your children, be careful to stress that we can't earn a new heart. God wants to give a new heart to everyone who repents and turns to him. That's good news!

A word of caution: It's not unusual for children raised in a Christian home to express a desire to become a Christian at an early age. As parents, it's sometimes hard to tell if a young child sincerely understands what it means to become a follower of Jesus.

If a young child asks you about becoming a Christian or about asking Jesus into his or her heart, how should you respond? Author and speaker Jim Elliff says we should be positive and encouraging, while at the same time challenging our child to live out the commitment he or she has made. He suggests saying something like this: "I'm thrilled that you are repenting and trusting in Christ. More than anything, we want to know that God has really changed your life. The way we will know is if you continue repenting and trusting and if you act like a true Christian—that is, you have a new heart that loves to obey God."

Ultimately, it is God who will call our children to come to him and know him. As parents, we should pray that God would draw our children to himself at an early age!

SESSION FIVE • LEARNING ABOUT GOD THROUGH JESUS CHRIST

Session Six

Responding to God

God takes the initiative in pursuing a relationship with our children and us, but a response is also called for.

WARM • UP   15 MINUTES

It Takes Two

Discuss these questions:

- When you first began developing a relationship with your spouse, which one of you was the primary pursuer in the relationship?
- If you were the pursuer, what is one of the things you did to attract the attention and interest of your spouse?
- If you were the pursued, what eventually caused you to respond to your spouse in a positive way?

Project Report

Share one thing you learned from last session's HomeBuilders Project.

BLUEPRINTS　　60 MINUTES

The Pursuer

In the Bible, God compares his relationship with us to a father's relationship with a child (Proverbs 3:11-12; Hebrews 12:5-11).

> If you have a large group, form smaller groups of about six people to answer the Blueprints questions. Unless otherwise noted, answer the questions in your sub-group. Before moving on to the Wrap-Up section, have subgroups report to the whole group the highlights from their discussions.

1. What do the following verses tell us about how God pursues a relationship with us?

- Psalm 139:7

- Ezekiel 34:16

- Luke 19:10

- 1 John 4:19

As you look back over your life, how have you seen God pursuing you?

2. What are some of the ways you hope or expect that your children will respond to you as you pursue a relationship with them?

Four Responses to God

The Scriptures provide us examples of ways we can respond to God. In the questions that follow we will explore four responses.

Love God

3. Read Matthew 22:36-37. What do you think it means to love God "with all your heart and with all your soul and with all your mind?"

SESSION SIX • RESPONDING TO GOD

4. What does love for God look like? Practically, in what ways can you model love for God to your children in everyday life?

Fear God

Fearing God means maintaining a reverential awe of the one who created heaven and earth and reigns as the supreme and sovereign ruler of the universe. One way to introduce this concept to your children is to read the book of Proverbs, which was written as a collection of wisdom passed down from a father to his son. Throughout Proverbs the author encourages his son to fear the Lord as he talks about the benefits that come from fearing the Lord.

5. Read Genesis 3:1-10 and Psalm 34:8-13. How is the "fear" of the Lord in Psalm 34 different from Adam's fear in the garden?

Answer question 6 with your spouse. After answering, you may want to share an appropriate insight or discovery with the group.

6. Select two or three of the following passages. What do these verses say about the benefits of fearing God? Discuss how you have experienced these benefits in your life and how you could explain them to your children.

- Proverbs 3:7-8

- Proverbs 19:23

- Proverbs 9:10

- Proverbs 22:4

- Proverbs 10:27

- Proverbs 28:14

- Proverbs 14:26-27

- Proverbs 31:30

- Proverbs 16:6

Trust God

Trusting God means having confidence in God's character and knowing that God is in control of our lives. It's a response that God calls for in times of trial and suffering.

7. Read Judges 7:1-7, 12. How do you think you would have reacted to Gideon's announcement in verse 3? What was Gideon's apparent response to his circumstances? Why do you think this was?

8. When are the times when we most need to put our trust in God and his plan? If you can, tell about an experience in which you or your children demonstrated trust in God.

9. What are some current situations in which your children need to trust in God's sovereignty right now? What can you do to encourage them?

Obey God

One tangible way for you and your children to demonstrate love, fear, and trust in God is to obey him. As Jesus said in John 14:15, "If you love me, you will obey what I command." All of us need to come to a place in our lives where our default response to God's commands is to obey rather than resist.

1 Samuel 15 tells the story of Saul, the king of Israel, who led his troops into battle and defeated the Amalekites. King Saul had been told by God to utterly destroy the Amalekites, but Saul did not obey. Verse 9

says, "But Saul and the army spared Agag and the best of the sheep and cattle, the fat calves and lambs—everything that was good. These they were unwilling to destroy completely, but everything that was despised and weak they totally destroyed." When the prophet Samuel came to Saul, he confronted him for failing to obey what God has commanded.

10. Read 1 Samuel 15:19-23. How did Saul respond when Samuel confronted him for not obeying God? What are common ways your children tend not to obey you fully? What are some typical responses from them when you confront their disobedience?

11. With each couple selecting one of the following scenarios, discuss how you could turn the situation into an opportunity to teach the child about the need to obey God. Then share your insights with the group.

• You see your five-year-old daughter stealing extra cookies from the kitchen pantry.

• You receive a phone call from the principal of your nine-year-old son's elementary school. The principal says your son has been forcing younger children to give him food from their lunches.

SESSION SIX • RESPONDING TO GOD

• You're concerned that your seventeen-year-old daughter is becoming too physically affectionate with her boyfriend. You talk with her about remaining sexually pure, and she asks, "Why is that so important? Lots of kids at school are doing it."

12. One way of helping your children see the need to obey God is by telling them about your own experiences. What's a recent situation in which you saw the need to obey God rather than follow your own desires?

HomeBuilder Principle:
Children need to be taught by you—in word and deed— to love, fear, trust, and obey God.

W R A P • U P   **15 MINUTES**

Looking Back, Looking Ahead

As you come to the end of this course, take a few
minutes to reflect on the experience. Review the following questions, and write down responses to the
questions you can answer. Then relate to the group
one or more of your answers.

- What has this group meant to you over the course
  of this study? Be specific.

- What is the most valuable thing that you have
  learned or discovered?

- How have you as a parent been changed or
  challenged?

SESSION SIX • RESPONDING TO GOD

- What would you like to see happen next for this group?

Make a Date

Make a date with your spouse to meet in the next week to complete the final HomeBuilders Project of this study.

_____
DATE

_____
TIME

_____
LOCATION

HOMEBUILDERS PROJECT　　　　6 0　M I N U T E S

As a Couple [10 minutes]

Congratulations—you've made it to the last project of this study! Start your date by reflecting on what impact this course has had on you by discussing these questions:

- What has been the best part of this study for you?
- How has this study benefited your marriage?
- In what ways has this course helped you as a parent?
- What is something new you've learned or discovered about yourself? your spouse? your children?

Individually [20 minutes]

1. What point from this session had the most impact on you and why?

2. Overall, what has been the most important insight or lesson for you from this course?

3. What is one step or action—something you want to do, stop doing, or change—that you identified during this course and that you need to follow through on? What needs to happen for this to become a reality?

SESSION SIX • RESPONDING TO GOD

4. In the group session, four different ways of responding to God—love, fear, trust, and obedience—were discussed. Which of these responses would you say comes easiest to you? which is the most difficult for you? Why do you think this is?

5. On a scale of 1 (poor) to 10 (good), how would you evaluate yourself for each of the following responses to God on how well you model these to your children?

___ love
___ fear
___ trust
___ obedience

Which of these responses do you think you need to emphasize more in your home? What is an example of one way you can think of to do this?

6. What, if anything, have you done recently that might lead your children to think that you don't love, trust, fear or obey God?

7. What is a situation you are facing right now that you could use as a teaching opportunity with your children to let them know how you are seeking to respond to God?

Interact as a Couple [30 minutes]

1. Share your answers from the individual section.

2. Thinking about each of your children, complete the chart that follows. Put your child's initials next to the situation(s) you have identified that specifically relates to him or her.

SESSION SIX • RESPONDING TO GOD

93

Situations that our children are facing that call for a response to...	How we can work with this child to encourage this response
Love God	
Fear God	
Trust God	
Obey God	

3. Evaluate what you can or should do or continue to do to strengthen your home. You may want to consider continuing the practice of setting aside time for date nights. Review the list of ideas on page 113.

4. Spend a few minutes in prayer together. Thank God for each other and for your children. Pray for God's wisdom, direction, and blessing as you continue to help your children know God.

Be sure to check out the Parent-Child Interaction on page 108.

Please visit our Web site at www.familylife.com/homebuilders to give us your feedback on this study and to get information on other FamilyLife resources and conferences.

Parent-Child Interactions

The object of each of these Parent-Child Interactions is to help parents connect with their children and help them know God. Make these a special occasion—perhaps as part of a weekly "Family Night."

Interaction 1

Celebrities

This project gives you the opportunity to tell your children how you came to know God. To make it a special night, plan a meal together—either a picnic, a family trip to a local fast-food restaurant, or a special meal at home. You can complete the following project at the end of the meal.

1. Give each child a blank sheet of paper (or make each child a copy of the "Celebrity Quiz" handout on page 98) and a pen or pencil.

2. Say: **For fun, we want to give you a quiz about famous people who mom and dad have met. To qualify as someone we've met, we must have either spoken to or shaken hands with the person. In each category, answer either true or false for both of us. If you answer true, write down the name of the famous person and earn one bonus point.**

3. Read the questions on the quiz, and have each child mark down answers.

PARENT-CHILD INTERACTIONS

97

Celebrity Quiz

- **I have met a *famous* movie or television star.**

    Mom   true / false
    Dad   true / false

- **I have met a local television personality, such as a news anchor, meteorologist, sportscaster, or reporter.**

    Mom   true / false
    Dad   true / false

- **I have met a professional athlete.**

    Mom   true / false
    Dad   true / false

- **I have met a politician.**

    Mom   true / false
    Dad   true / false

- **I have met a well-known author or musician.**

    Mom   true / false
    Dad   true / false

- **I have met God.**

    Mom   true / false
    Dad   true / false

4. Now go back through the questions, and tell your children the correct answers. For each true answer, explain the circumstances of how you met the person, who introduced you, and how you felt about meeting the person. For the last question, take time to share your faith story—how you became a follower of Jesus.

5. Conclude by asking your children if they know when and how they were first introduced to God.

Interaction 2

Looking for Evidence

This project helps children see that they can learn about God by looking at his creation. The main activity needs to take place outdoors—at a park or a favorite outdoor recreation site, for example. You will need a disposable camera and a paper bag for each child.

1. Give each child a disposable camera (or to save a little money, have your children share a camera) and a paper bag. Read aloud Jeremiah 32:17 and Romans 1:20. Explain that we can learn about God by observing what he has created.

2. Say: **Today you're going to be detectives and look for evidence that God has been here. Here's your assignment:**

- **Gather five pieces of evidence from nature that show us something about God, and put them in your bag.**

- **Take pictures of at least five other things that you see as evidence of God.**

3. After your children have finished, have the film developed at a one-hour developing service. Then have your children take turns presenting their evidence and making a case that God had been at the place of your family outing.

During your children's presentations, look for opportunities to ask questions to help them prove their case. For example, when a child shows you a leaf, ask: **How does this help prove God was in the park?**

Help your children understand that only God can make a leaf. You may want to say: **A scientist can't create one in a laboratory. A builder can't build one in a workshop. A person who sews can't make a leaf on a sewing machine. Only God can make a leaf.**

PARENT-CHILD INTERACTIONS

4. After the presentations have been made, ask these questions:

- **What does the evidence that was presented teach us about God?**
- **What kind of God can make these things?**

5. End this interaction by praying together. Thank God for the things he has made.

Interaction 3

Home Movies

Kids love making home movies and acting out stories. Plan a night to videotape your own epic motion picture based on a biblical story with your children as actors.

1. If you don't have a video camera, make arrangements to borrow one. (Another option would be to photograph movie "scenes" rather than making a movie.)

2. Select a story to shoot. Here are some options to consider:

- Jacob wrestles with an angel—Genesis 32:22
- Zacchaeus and Jesus—Luke 19
- The woman at the well—John 4
- Jesus and the disciples in the boat during the storm— Matthew 8:23
- Jesus heals a woman—Luke 8:43
- The Prodigal Son—Luke 15:11
- David and Goliath—1 Samuel 17
- Jesus at Mary and Martha's house—Luke 10:38
- Daniel in the Lions' Den—Daniel 6

3. Read through the story (probably more than once), and talk about how to make it into a movie. Decide:

- who will play each character, keeping in mind that someone can play more than one character in the story. For example, someone who plays King Darius in the story of Daniel can also be a lion! Also remember that someone needs to be videotaping each scene.
- what costumes and props you need.
- where each scene will be filmed.

PARENT-CHILD INTERACTIONS

101

4. Shoot your movie. At the end, ask each of the actors to respond on camera to this question: **What did I learn about God from this story?**

5. Pop some popcorn, and watch your movie.

Be careful with this. Your children may want to make a movie every night!

Interaction 4

Bread of Life

This is a slightly different version of the learning exercise you did as a group in Session Four. This interaction provides a memorable lesson about one of the descriptions that we find in Scripture about Jesus.

1. Delay dinner (or lunch) by two or three hours to ensure that everyone in your family is very hungry. Don't allow anyone to eat any snacks during this time.

2. To begin your meal, give a piece of bread (preferably some type of whole-grain bread) to each person. Encourage them to eat it. Ask:

- **How does this bread taste to you when you're this hungry?**

- **How does it normally taste to you?**

- **If you went twenty-four hours without food, how do you think this piece of bread would taste?**

3. Read John 6:35 and then ask: **What do you think Jesus means when he says, "I am the bread of life. He who comes to me will never go hungry"?**

4. Talk about the fact that bread provides some of the protein, complex carbohydrates, vitamins, iron, fiber, and other nutrients that we need to live. But Jesus is talking about something different—he satisfies us spiritually. Jesus gives us what our souls need to survive.

5. Read Deuteronomy 8:3. Ask: **What does this verse tell us about what we need to live?**

6. Share with your children how God's Word has helped you grow closer to God.

PARENT-CHILD INTERACTIONS

103

Interaction 5

A New Heart

This project gives you the opportunity to tell your children about their need for a "new heart"—which we receive when we become believers in Christ. You will need Bibles, paper, and either pencils, pens, or crayons for each child. Also, you will need to create two birthday party invitations. The date and time for each party should be the same—your children will be asked to choose which one they want to attend. One invitation should look like a child's party invitation—no frills. The second invitation should be on fancy paper with text similar to the sample below:

World's Greatest Birthday Party!

Enjoy a day of fun at _____!

*[Fill in the name of a local amusement park, water park, or
other place that is popular with children.]*

All the hamburgers, pizza, and ice cream and cake you can eat!

Everyone attending the party receives:

a FREE laptop computer,

a FREE TV,

a free DVD player,

a $1,000 gift certificate for the mall, and...

A FREE CAR WHEN YOU TURN 16!

---

1. Give each child a blank sheet of paper and something to draw with. Say: **Today we're going to talk about the need each of us has for a new heart. So the first thing I want each of you to do is draw a picture of a heart.**

2. After each child has created a heart, ask: **What does your heart stand for? What does it symbolize to you?**

3. Say: **When we think of a heart, we also think of the one inside the body.** Have them each feel for their heartbeats by putting their hands on the left side of their chests or by feeling their pulse on their wrists. Ask:

- **What does the heart do for us?**

- **What would happen if our heart stopped beating?**

4. Say: **When the Bible talks about a person's heart, it usually means something a bit different.** Assign your children to find and read aloud the following passages:

- Deuteronomy 5:29

- Psalm 5:9

- Psalm 53:1

- Matthew 15:18-19

- Matthew 22:37

5. Ask: **What do you think the Bible means when it talks about the heart?** This may be a difficult question for your children to answer, but let them grapple with it for a little while, and then say: **In the Bible the heart represents the core of a person. It's the center of thoughts, emotions, and desires. It determines how we behave. This may be hard to understand, so I'm going to illustrate with these two birthday invitations.**

6. Display the invitation for the party with the free gifts, and say: **Imagine that you have been invited to two birthday parties, but both parties are on the same day and at the same time. The first invitation comes from someone in your class at school who is your worst enemy. This child is a bully who picks on you and steals your lunch every day.** Read the invitation.

PARENT-CHILD INTERACTIONS **105**

7. Now show your child the other invitation. Say: **This invitation is from your best friend. The party will be held at the park, and you will play games, eat ice cream and cake, and watch your friend open presents. There are no promises of extravagant gifts—just the promise of a fun day with your friends. You can only attend one of these parties.** Ask: **Which one would you choose?**

8. Let your children wrestle with this decision for a couple of minutes. Then ask: **Why would you think of going to the party of your worst enemy at school?** The common answer will likely be "for the gifts!" Then ask:

- **Why would you think of giving up all those great gifts so you could go to your best friend's party?**

- **Do you think your best friend's feelings would be hurt if you chose to go to the other party?**

9. Say: **One of these choices would be self-motivated and the other would be a selfless choice.** Then ask: **How many of you secretly wish you could perhaps find a way to go to that party and get all those goodies?** After they answer, say: **Here's the point:** *The fact that we're tempted to go to the party where we will get all those things even though it would hurt the feelings of a best friend shows what our hearts are like—we're naturally selfish.* **Each of us is naturally selfish and sinful. We want our own way.**

10. Ask: **What are some of the ways that we show this selfishness?**

11. Have a child read Psalm 51:10. Then ask: **How do you think we can get a pure heart?**

12. Say: **The fact is that we have to get rid of our old, sinful heart and replace it with a new heart. The Bible tells us that this is why Christ came.** Have a child read Romans 5:8. Then say: **Imagine that your doctor has just told you that you have a diseased heart and that unless you receive a heart transplant very soon your sick heart will kill you. Because of your type of blood and cells in your body, there is only one person who is a match for you as a donor. But in order for you to live, this person would have to be willing to give up his life for yours. There is nothing you can do to save yourself.**

Ask: **What would you think if this person came willingly and offered to give you his heart so that you might live?** After they answer, say: **This is what Jesus came to do for us. Jesus died so that we might have a new heart.**

PARENT-CHILD INTERACTIONS

107

Interaction 6

Invitations

For this particular family night, you'll need to create six to eight invitation cards. You can create these invitations by hand with construction paper and some markers or by using your computer.

The cover of each invitation should read "You're Invited!" But on the inside, be creative about the type of event taking place (see the examples that follow). Make up a date and time for each event. You might also include what to bring. On the inside, at the bottom of most of the invitations, write, "This invitation is pretend." For one or two of the invitations (like the pizza invitation), write the words, "This invitation is real. You can cash it in for pizza on the night of your choice. Congratulations!"

Sample Invitations

You're Invited!

What: Traffic Court

Who: The Judge

When: Next Wednesday at 6:30 p.m.

What to bring: Some money to pay your fine—or else!

RSVP!

You're Invited!

What: Lunch at the White House

Who: The President

When: In June

What to bring: Your ideas about how to improve the country

RSVP!

HELPING YOUR CHILDREN KNOW GOD

You're Invited!

What: Kitchen cleanup duty

Who: Mom and Dad

When: Every night this week

What to bring: Detergent, rubber gloves, and a broom

RSVP!

You're Invited!

What: Pizza

Who: The whole family

When: You pick the night

What to bring: Your appetite!

RSVP!

For Extra Impact:
You may also want to create in advance a special invitation for each of your children from God, inviting them to know him. If you do this, pass these out when you get to the last question under point number four.

You're Invited!

What: Dinner at my house

Who: The Big Bad Wolf

When: The sooner the better

What to bring: Just yourself!

RSVP!

1. Lay the invitations you made facedown on the kitchen table. Tell each child to select one, one at a time. But *before* your children open or look at the invitation, ask:

- **Why did you pick the invitation you selected?**
- **Are you willing to do what this invitation asks?**

PARENT-CHILD INTERACTIONS

Make each child decide yes or no before opening the invitation. Once your children open and read (or have read to them) their invitations, ask: **Do you want to stick by the choice you made before you opened the invitation, or do you want to change your mind?**

2. Once you've looked through all the invitations, turn in the Bible to Luke 14:16-24. Read the story, then discuss the following questions as a family:

- **Why do you think some of the people didn't want to come to the king's banquet?**

- **Does it sound like they had valid reasons why they could not come, or were they just making excuses? Explain.**

- **Who were the people who came to the king's banquet?**

- **If you received an invitation to the king's banquet, would you want to attend? Why or why not?**

3. Explain to your children that Jesus' point in this story is that all of us have been invited to know God and to have a relationship with him. Many people who receive that invitation make excuses for not following Jesus. But God has room for anyone who will come.

4. Ask:

- **What are some reasons why people might not want to know God or have a relationship with him?**

- **What are some reasons why people would choose to say yes to God's invitation?**

- **What do you think about God's invitation to us to know him better?**

5. Close your time in prayer. Thank God for his invitation to us to be his followers!

Where Do You Go From Here?

It is our prayer that you have benefited greatly from this study in the HomeBuilders Parenting Series. We hope that your marriage and home will continue to grow stronger as you both submit your lives to Jesus Christ and build according to his blueprints.

We also hope that you will begin reaching out to strengthen other marriages in your community and local church. Your church needs couples like you who are committed to building Christian marriages. A favorite World War II story illustrates this point very clearly.

The year was 1940. The French Army had just collapsed under Hitler's onslaught. The Dutch had folded, overwhelmed by the Nazi regime. The Belgians had surrendered. And the British Army was trapped on the coast of France in the channel port of Dunkirk.

Two hundred and twenty thousand of Britain's finest young men seemed doomed to die, turning the English Channel red with their blood. The Fuehrer's troops, only miles away in the hills of France, didn't realize how close to victory they actually were.

Any rescue seemed feeble and futile in the time remaining. A "thin" British Navy—"the professionals"—told King George VI that at best they could save 17,000 troops. The House of Commons was warned to prepare for "hard and heavy tidings."

Politicians were paralyzed. The king was powerless. And the Allies could only watch as spectators from a distance. Then as the doom of the British Army seemed imminent, a strange fleet appeared on the horizon of the English Channel—the wildest assortment of boats perhaps ever assembled in history.

Trawlers, tugs, scows, fishing sloops, lifeboats, pleasure craft, smacks and coasters, sailboats, even the London fire-brigade flotilla. *Each ship was manned by civilian volunteers—English fathers sailing to rescue Britain's exhausted, bleeding sons.*

William Manchester writes in his epic book, *The Last Lion*, that even today what happened in 1940 in less than twenty-four hours seems like a miracle—not only were all of the British soldiers rescued, but 118,000 other Allied troops as well.

Today the Christian home is much like those troops at Dunkirk. Pressured, trapped, and demoralized, it needs help. Your help. The Christian community may be much like England—we stand waiting for politicians, professionals, even for our pastors to step in and save the family. But the problem is much larger than all of those combined can solve.

With the highest divorce rate of any nation on earth, we need an all-out effort by men and women who are determined to help rescue the exhausted and wounded casualties of today's families. We need an outreach effort by common couples with faith in an uncommon God.

May we challenge you to invest your lives in others? You have one of the greatest opportunities in history—to help save today's families. By starting a HomeBuilders group, you can join couples around the world who are building and rebuilding hundreds of thousands of homes with a new, solid foundation of a relationship with God.

Will You Join Us in "Touching Lives...Changing Families"?

The following are some practical ways you can make a difference in families today:

1. Gather a group of four to eight couples, and lead them through the six sessions of this HomeBuilders study, *Helping Your Children Know God.* (Why not consider challenging others in your church or community to form additional HomeBuilders groups?)

2. Commit to continue building your marriage and home by doing another course in the HomeBuilders Parenting Series or by leading a study in the HomeBuilders Couples Series.

3. An excellent outreach tool is the film *JESUS,* which is available on video. For more information, contact FamilyLife at 1-800-FL-TODAY.

4. Host a dinner party. Invite families from your neighborhood to your home, and as a couple share your faith in Christ.

5. Reach out and share the love of Christ with neighborhood children.

6. If you have attended the Weekend to Remember conference, why not offer to assist your pastor in counseling couples engaged to be married, using the material you received?

For more information about any of the above ministry opportunities, contact your local church, or write:

> **FamilyLife**
> P.O. Box 8220
> Little Rock, AR 72221-8220
> 1-800-FL-TODAY
> **www.familylife.com**

Our Problems, God's Answers

Every couple eventually has to deal with problems in marriage. Communication problems. Parenting issues. Money problems. Difficulties with sexual intimacy. These issues are important to cultivating a strong, loving relationship with your spouse. HomeBuilders Bible studies are designed to help you strengthen your marriage and family in many of these critical areas.

Part One: The Big Problem

One basic problem is at the heart of every other problem in every marriage, and it's a problem we can't help you fix. No matter how hard you try, this is one problem that is too big for you to deal with on your own.

The problem is separation from God. If you want to experience marriage the way it was designed to be, you need a vital relationship with the God who created you and offers you the power to live a life of joy and purpose.

And what separates us from God is one more problem—sin. Most of us have assumed throughout our lives that the term "sin" refers to a list of bad habits that everyone agrees are wrong. We try to deal with our sin problem by working hard to become better people. We read books to learn how to control our anger, or we resolve to stop cheating on our taxes.

But in our hearts, we know our sin problem runs much deeper than a list of bad habits. All of us have rebelled against God. We have ignored him and have decided to run our own lives in a way that makes sense to us. The Bible says that the God who created us wants us to follow his plan for our lives. But because of our sin problem, we think our ideas and plans are better than his.

- *"For all have sinned and fall short of the glory of God"* (Romans 3:23).

What does it mean to "fall short of the glory of God"? It means that none of us has trusted and treasured God the way we should. We have sought to satisfy ourselves with other things and have treated those things as more valuable than God. We have gone our own way. According to the Bible, we have to pay a penalty for our sin. We cannot simply do things the way we choose and hope it will all be OK with God. Following our own plan leads to our destruction.

- *"There is a way that seems right to a man, but in the end it leads to death"* (Proverbs 14:12).

- *"For the wages of sin is death"* (Romans 6:23a).

The penalty for sin is that we are forever separated from God's love. God is holy, and we are sinful. No matter how hard we try, we cannot come up with some plan, like living a good life or even trying to do what the Bible says, and hope that we can avoid the penalty.

God's Solution to Sin

Thankfully, God has a way to solve our dilemma. He became a man through the person of Jesus Christ. He lived a holy life, in perfect obedience to God's plan. He also willingly died on a cross to pay our penalty for sin. Then he proved that he is more powerful than sin or death by rising from the dead. He alone has the power to overrule the penalty for our sin.

OUR PROBLEMS, GOD'S ANSWERS

- *"Jesus answered, 'I am the way and the truth and the life. No one comes to the Father except through me' "* (John 14:6).

- *"But God demonstrates his own love for us in this: While we were still sinners, Christ died for us"* (Romans 5:8).

- *"Christ died for our sins...he was buried...he was raised on the third day according to the Scriptures...he appeared to Peter, and then to the Twelve. After that, he appeared to more than five hundred"* (1 Corinthians 15:3-6).

- *"For the wages of sin is death, but the gift of God is eternal life in Christ Jesus our Lord"* (Romans 6:23).

The death of Jesus has fixed our sin problem. He has bridged the gap between God and us. He is calling all of us to come to him and to give up our own flawed plan for how to run our lives. He wants us to trust God and his plan.

Accepting God's Solution

If you agree that you are separated from God, he is calling you to confess your sins. All of us have made messes of our lives because we have stubbornly preferred our ideas and plans over his. As a result, we deserve to be cut off from God's love and his care for us. But God has promised that if we will agree that we have rebelled against his plan for us and have messed up our lives, he will forgive us and will fix our sin problem.

- *"Yet to all who received him, to those who believed in his name, he gave the right to become children of God"* (John 1:12).

- *"For it is by grace you have been saved, through faith—and this not from yourselves, it is the gift of*

God—not by works, so that no one can boast" (Ephesians 2:8-9).

When the Bible talks about receiving Christ, it means we acknowledge that we are sinners and that we can't fix the problem ourselves. It means we turn away from our sin. And it means we trust Christ to forgive our sins and to make us the kind of people he wants us to be. It's not enough to just intellectually believe that Christ is the Son of God. We must trust in him and his plan for our lives by faith, as an act of the will.

Are things right between you and God, with him and his plan at the center of your life? Or is life spinning out of control as you seek to make your way on your own?

You can decide today to make a change. You can turn to Christ and allow him to transform your life. All you need to do is to talk to him and tell him what is stirring in your mind and in your heart. If you've never done this before, consider taking the steps listed here:

- Do you agree that you need God? Tell God.

- Have you made a mess of your life by following your own plan? Tell God.

- Do you want God to forgive you? Tell God.

- Do you believe that Jesus' death on the cross and his resurrection from the dead gave him the power to fix your sin problem and to grant you the gift of eternal life? Tell God.

- Are you ready to acknowledge that God's plan for your life is better than any plan you could come up with? Tell God.

- Do you agree that God has the right to be the Lord and master of your life? Tell God.

"Seek the Lord while he may be found;
call on him while he is near"
(Isaiah 55:6).

Following is a suggested prayer:

Lord Jesus, I need you. Thank you for dying on the
cross for my sins. I receive you as my Savior and Lord.
Thank you for forgiving my sins and giving me eternal
life. Make me the kind of person you want me to be.

Does this prayer express the desire of your heart? If it
does, pray it right now, and Christ will come into your life, as
he promised.

Part Two: Living the Christian Life

For a person who is a follower of Christ—a Christian—the
penalty for sin is paid in full. But the effect of sin continues
throughout our lives.

- *"If we claim to be without sin, we deceive ourselves*
  and the truth is not in us" (1 John 1:8).

- *"For what I do is not the good I want to do; no,*
  the evil I do not want to do—this I keep on doing"
  (Romans 7:19).

The effects of sin carry over into our marriages as well. Even
Christians struggle to maintain solid, God-honoring marriages.
Most couples eventually realize that they can't do it on their
own. But with God's help, they can succeed. The Holy Spirit
can have a huge impact in the marriages of Christians who live
constantly, moment by moment, under his gracious direction.

Self-Centered Christians

Many Christians struggle to live the Christian life in their own strength because they are not allowing God to control their lives. Their interests are self-directed, often resulting in failure and frustration.

- *"Brothers, I could not address you as spiritual but as worldly—mere infants in Christ. I gave you milk, not solid food, for you were not yet ready for it. Indeed, you are still not ready. You are still worldly. For since there is jealousy and quarreling among you, are you not worldly? Are you not acting like mere men?"* (1 Corinthians 3:1-3).

The self-centered Christian cannot experience the abundant and fruitful Christian life. Such people trust in their own efforts to live the Christian life: They are either uninformed about—or have forgotten—God's love, forgiveness, and power. This kind of Christian

- has an up-and-down spiritual experience.

- cannot understand himself—he wants to do what is right, but cannot.

- fails to draw upon the power of the Holy Spirit to live the Christian life.

Some or all of the following traits may characterize the Christian who does not fully trust God:

disobedience	plagued by impure thoughts
lack of love for God and others	jealous
	worrisome
inconsistent prayer life	easily discouraged, frustrated
lack of desire for Bible study	critical
legalistic attitude	lack of purpose

OUR PROBLEMS, GOD'S ANSWERS

Note: The individual who professes to be a Christian but who continues to practice sin should realize that he may not be a Christian at all, according to Ephesians 5:5 and 1 John 2:3; 3:6, 9.

Spirit-Centered Christians

When a Christian puts Christ on the throne of his life, he yields to God's control. This Christian's interests are directed by the Holy Spirit, resulting in harmony with God's plan.

- *"But the fruit of the Spirit is love, joy, peace, patience, kindness, goodness, faithfulness, gentleness and self-control. Against such things there is no law"* (Galatians 5:22-23).

Jesus said:

- *"I have come that they may have life, and have it to the full"* (John 10:10b).

- *"I am the vine; you are the branches. If a man remains in me and I in him, he will bear much fruit; apart from me you can do nothing"* (John 15:5).

- *"But you will receive power when the Holy Spirit comes on you; and you will be my witnesses in Jerusalem, and in all Judea and Samaria, and to the ends of the earth"* (Acts 1:8).

The following traits result naturally from the Holy Spirit's work in our lives:

Christ centered	love
Holy Spirit empowered	joy
motivated to tell others about Jesus	peace
	patience
dedicated to prayer	kindness
student of God's Word	goodness
trusts God	faithfulness
obeys God	gentleness
	self-control

The degree to which these traits appear in a Christian's life and marriage depends upon the extent to which the Christian trusts the Lord with every detail of life, and upon that person's maturity in Christ. One who is only beginning to understand the ministry of the Holy Spirit should not be discouraged if he is not as fruitful as mature Christians who have known and experienced this truth for a longer period of time.

Giving God Control

Jesus promises his followers an abundant and fruitful life as they allow themselves to be directed and empowered by the Holy Spirit. As we give God control of our lives, Christ lives in and through us in the power of the Holy Spirit (John 15).

If you sincerely desire to be directed and empowered by God, you can turn your life over to the control of the Holy Spirit right now (Matthew 5:6; John 7:37-39).

First, confess your sins to God, agreeing with him that you want to turn from any past sinful patterns in your life. Thank God in faith that he has forgiven all of your sins because Christ died

OUR PROBLEMS, GOD'S ANSWERS

for you (Colossians 2:13-15; 1 John 1:9; 2:1-3; Hebrews 10:1-18).

Be sure to offer every area of your life to God (Romans 12:1-2). Consider what areas you might rather keep to yourself, and be sure you're willing to give God control in those areas.

By faith, commit yourself to living according to the Holy Spirit's guidance and power.

- *Live by the Spirit:* **"So I say, live by the Spirit, and you will not gratify the desires of the sinful nature. For the sinful nature desires what is contrary to the Spirit, and the Spirit what is contrary to the sinful nature. They are in conflict with each other, so that you do not do what you want"** (Galatians 5:16-17).

- *Trust in God's promise:* **"This is the confidence we have in approaching God: that if we ask anything according to his will, he hears us. And if we know that he hears us—whatever we ask—we know that we have what we asked of him"** (1 John 5:14-15).

Expressing Your Faith Through Prayer

Prayer is one way of expressing your faith to God. If the prayer that follows expresses your sincere desire, consider praying the prayer or putting the thoughts into your own words:

> **Dear God, I need you. I acknowledge that I have been directing my own life and that, as a result, I have sinned against you. I thank you that you have forgiven my sins through Christ's death on the cross for me. I now invite Christ to take his place on the throne of my life. Take control of my life through the Holy Spirit as you promised you would if I asked in faith. I now thank you for directing my life and for empowering me through the Holy Spirit.**

Walking in the Spirit

If you become aware of an area of your life (an attitude or an action) that is displeasing to God, simply confess your sin, and thank God that he has forgiven your sins on the basis of Christ's death on the cross. Accept God's love and forgiveness by faith, and continue to have fellowship with him.

If you find that you've taken back control of your life through sin—a definite act of disobedience—try this exercise, "Spiritual Breathing," as you give that control back to God.

1. Exhale. Confess your sin. Agree with God that you've sinned against him, and thank him for his forgiveness of it, according to 1 John 1:9 and Hebrews 10:1-25. Remember that confession involves repentance, a determination to change attitudes and actions.

2. Inhale. Surrender control of your life to Christ, inviting the Holy Spirit to once again take charge. Trust that he now directs and empowers you, according to the command of Galatians 5:16-17 and the promise of 1 John 5:14-15. Returning to your faith in God enables you to continue to experience God's love and forgiveness.

Revolutionizing Your Marriage

This new commitment of your life to God will enrich your marriage. Sharing with your spouse what you've committed to is a powerful step in solidifying this commitment. As you exhibit the Holy Spirit's work within you, your spouse may be drawn to make the same commitment you've made. If both of you have given control of your lives to the Holy Spirit, you'll be able to help each other remain true to God, and your marriage may be revolutionized. With God in charge of your lives, life becomes an amazing adventure.

Leader Notes

Contents

About Leading a HomeBuilders Group **125**

About the Leader Notes...**128**

Session One **129**

Session Two **133**

Session Three **135**

Session Four **137**

Session Five..**139**

Session Six **142**

About Leading a HomeBuilders Group

What is the leader's job?

Your role is that of "facilitator"—one who encourages people to think and to discover what Scripture says, who helps group members feel comfortable, and who keeps things moving forward.

What is the best setting and time schedule for this study?

This study is designed as a small-group home Bible study. However, it can be adapted for use in a Sunday school setting as well. Here are some suggestions for using this study in a small group and in a Sunday school class:

In a small group

To create a friendly and comfortable atmosphere, it is recommended that you do this study in a home setting. In many cases, the couple that leads the study also serves as host to the group. Sometimes involving another couple as host is a good idea. Choose the option you believe will work best for your group, taking into account factors such as the number of couples participating and the location.

Each session is designed as a ninety-minute study, but we recommend a two-hour block of time. This will allow you to move through each part of the study at a more relaxed pace. However, be sure to keep in mind one of the cardinal rules of a small group: Good groups start *and* end on time. People's time is valuable, and your group will appreciate your being respectful of this.

In a Sunday school class

There are two important adaptations you need to make if you

LEADER NOTES

want to use this study in a class setting: (1) The material you cover should focus on the content from the Blueprints section of each session. Blueprints is the heart of each session and is designed to last sixty minutes. (2) Most Sunday school classes are taught in a teacher format instead of a small-group format. If this study will be used in a class setting, the class should adapt to a small-group dynamic. This will involve an interactive, discussion-based format and may also require a class to break into multiple smaller groups (we recommend groups of six to eight people).

What is the best size group?

We recommend from four to eight couples (including you and your spouse). If you have more people interested than you think you can accommodate, consider asking someone else to lead a second group. If you have a large group, you are encouraged at various times in the study to break into smaller subgroups. This helps you cover the material in a timely fashion and allows for optimum interaction and participation within the group.

What about refreshments?

Many groups choose to serve refreshments, which help create an environment of fellowship. If you plan on including refreshments in your study, here are a couple of suggestions: (1) For the first session (or two) you should provide the refreshments and then allow the group to be involved by having people sign up to bring them on later dates. (2) Consider starting your group with a short time of informal fellowship and refreshments (fifteen minutes), then move into the study. If couples are late, they miss only the food and don't disrupt the study. You may also want to have refreshments available at the end of your meeting to encourage fellowship, but remember, respect the group members' time by ending the study on schedule and allowing anyone who needs to leave right away the opportunity to do so gracefully.

What about child care?

Groups handle this differently depending on their needs. Here are a couple of options you may want to consider:

- Have group members be responsible for making their own arrangements.
- As a group, hire child care, and have all the kids watched in one location.

What about prayer?

An important part of a small group is prayer. However, as the leader, you need to be sensitive to the level of comfort the people in your group have toward praying in front of others. Never call on people to pray aloud if you don't know if they are comfortable doing this. There are a number of creative approaches you can take, such as modeling prayer, calling for volunteers, and letting people state their prayers in the form of finishing a sentence. A tool that is helpful in a group is a prayer list. You are encouraged to utilize a prayer list, but let it be someone else's ministry to the group. You should lead the prayer time, but allow another couple in the group the opportunity to create, update, and distribute prayer lists.

In closing

An excellent resource that covers leading a HomeBuilders group in greater detail is the *HomeBuilders Leader Guide* by Drew and Kit Coons. This book may be obtained at your local Christian bookstore or by contacting Group Publishing or FamilyLife.

LEADER NOTES

About the Leader Notes

The sessions in this study can be easily led without a lot of preparation time. However, accompanying Leader Notes have been provided to assist you in preparation. The categories within the Leader Notes are as follows:

Objectives

The purpose of the Objectives is to help focus on the issues that will be presented in each session.

Notes and Tips

This section will relate any general comments about the session. This information should be viewed as ideas, helps, and suggestions. You may want to create a checklist of things you want to be sure to do in each session.

Commentary

Included in this section are notes that relate specifically to Blueprints questions. Not all Blueprints questions in each session will have accompanying commentary notes. Questions with related commentaries are designated by numbers (for example, Blueprints question 5 in Session One would correspond to number 5 in the Commentary section of Session One Leader Notes).

| Leader Notes |

Session One:
Getting to Know God

Objectives

Our primary assignment as parents is to show our children how they can know God.

In this session parents will

- reflect on how they viewed God as a child and what influences shaped their view of God.
- compare the process of introducing someone to introducing their children to God.
- recognize their crucial role in helping their children know God.
- get to know others in the group.

Notes and Tips

1. Welcome to the first session of the HomeBuilders course *Helping Your Children Know God.* While it's anticipated that most of the participants in this HomeBuilders Parenting Series study will be couples with children, be aware that you may have single parents, future parents, or even one parent from a marriage participating. Welcome everyone warmly, and work to create a supportive and encouraging environment.

You'll find certain features throughout this study that are specifically geared toward couples, such as designated couples questions and the HomeBuilders Projects. However, we encourage you as the leader to be flexible and sensitive to your group. For example, if you have a single parent in your group, you might invite that person to join you and your spouse when a couple's question is indicated in the study.

LEADER NOTES **129**

Or, if there are a number of single parents, you may want to encourage them to join together for these questions. Likewise, for the HomeBuilders Project at the end of every session, you may want to encourage singles to complete what they can individually or to work with another single parent on the project.

2. If you have not already done so, you will want to read the "About the Sessions" information on pages 4 and 5, as well as "About Leading a HomeBuilders Group" and "About the Leader Notes" starting on page 125.

3. As part of the first session, review with the group some Ground Rules (see page 11 in the Introduction).

4. Be sure you have a study guide for each person. You'll also want to have extra Bibles and pens or pencils.

5. Depending on the size of your group, you may spend longer than fifteen minutes on the Warm-Up section. If this happens, try to finish the Blueprints section in forty-five to sixty minutes. It's a good idea to mark the questions in Blueprints that you want to be sure to cover. Encourage couples to look at any questions you don't get to during the session when they do the HomeBuilders Project for this session.

6. You'll notice a note in the margin at the start of the Blueprints section that recommends breaking into smaller groups. The reason for this is twofold: (1) to help facilitate discussion and participation by everyone, and (2) to help you be able to get through the material in the allotted time.

7. Throughout the sessions in this course, you will find questions that are designed for spouses to answer together (like questions 4 and 12 in this session). The purpose of these "couples questions" is to foster communication and unity between spouses and give couples an opportunity to deal with personal issues. While couples are free to share their responses to these questions with the group, respect that not all couples will want to do so.

8. With this group just getting under way, it's not too late to invite another couple to join the group. During Wrap-Up, challenge everyone to think about someone they could invite to the next session.

9. Before dismissing, make a special point to tell the group about the importance of the HomeBuilders Project. Encourage each couple to "Make a Date" before the next meeting to complete this session's project. Mention that you'll ask about their experience with the project at the next session.

In addition to the HomeBuilders Projects, there are six Parent-Child Interactions (starting on page 97). These are designed to help give parents an opportunity to communicate with their children. Though we recommend that parents try and complete the interactions between sessions, we know that this will be a challenge. We encourage couples to place a priority on first completing the HomeBuilders Projects and then doing the Parent-Child Interactions when they have time, whether between sessions or at a later date.

Commentary

Here is some additional information related to select Blueprints questions. The numbers that follow correspond to the Blueprints questions of the same numbers in the session. Notes are not included for every question, as many of the questions in this study are designed for group members to draw from their own opinions and experiences. If you share any of these points, be sure to do so in a manner that does not stifle discussion by making you the authority with the "real answers." Keep in mind that these sessions are designed around group interaction and participation.

LEADER NOTES **131**

1. A potential follow up question to ask: What are one or two perceptions your children have about God?

5. Parents are given the responsibility to teach the Scriptures to their children and encourage them to set their hope in God, remember the works of God, and keep his commandments. Children who do not learn this will grow up to be stubborn and rebellious.

7. Information sources could include a variety of credible sources, such as various public records as well as firsthand information from close friends and family members.

10. In the process of introducing our children to God, we need to use the Bible, the most credible source of information about God and who he is. We need to meet with others who have many years of experience of walking with the Lord and learn from them. And we need to tell our children how we came to know God and what we have learned, putting it in words they can understand.

11. A part of the process illustrated in this passage is that these men stopped what they were doing and followed Jesus. The people in this passage who introduced Jesus to others met Jesus and were therefore qualified to help others come to know him in the same way they did.

Attention HomeBuilders Leaders

FamilyLife invites you to register your HomeBuilders group. Your registration connects you to the HomeBuilders Leadership Network, a worldwide movement of couples who are using HomeBuilders to strengthen marriages and families in their communities. You'll receive the latest news about HomeBuilders and other ministry opportunities to help strengthen marriages and families in your community. As the HomeBuilders Leadership Network grows, we'll offer additional resources such as online training, prayer requests, and chats with authors. There's no cost or obligation to register; simply go to www.familylife.com/homebuilders.

Leader Notes

Session Two:
Getting to Know God Through Creation

Objectives

Our children can learn about God from his creation.

In this session parents will

- explore some of the evidence God gives us about his character through creation.
- talk about how they can use God's creation to teach their children about God.
- examine another way God has revealed himself—through our God-given conscience.

Notes and Tips

1. Because this is the second session, your group members have probably warmed up to one another but may not yet feel free to be completely open about their relationships. Don't force the issue. Continue to encourage couples to attend and to complete the projects.

2. If new people join the group this session, during Warm-Up ask them to introduce themselves to the group and to share the names and ages of their children. Also give a brief summary of the main points from Session One, and have the group pass around their books to record contact information (p. 14).

3. Make sure the arrangements for refreshments (if you're planning to have them) are covered.

4. If your group has decided to use a prayer list, make sure this is covered.

LEADER NOTES

5. If you told the group during the first session that you'd be asking them about the first HomeBuilders Project, be sure to do so. This is an opportunity to establish an environment of accountability. However, be prepared to share a report of your own about the project from the first session.

6. Question 7 in Blueprints calls for couples to look up different Scripture passages. This approach allows people to simultaneously examine multiple passages. This saves time and gives group members the chance to learn from one another.

7. For the closing prayer in this session, you may want to ask for a volunteer or two to close the group in prayer.

Commentary

Note: The numbers that follow correspond to the Blueprints questions of the same numbers in the session.

6. Some of the things revealed to us about God by these things: He is very creative and not limited by size, number, or distance. He has great power. He is interested in minute details.

7. Through his creation, God gives us something physical and real to help us understand him. Some of the insights from these verses include: God is the creator. God is all-powerful—nothing is too hard for him. God's power and divine nature can be known through creation. God is love.

9. We enter this world with an innate knowledge and desire to sin. If we are not trained in what is good, we will gravitate toward the thoughts and acts of self-centered sin. We do have a conscience, the Law of God written on our hearts, but we do not usually respond to our conscience without outside instruction or guidance.

10. Some examples include acts such as murder, stealing, and adultery.

11. Our conscience is God-given and is a tool God uses in relating to us.

| Leader Notes |

Session Three:
Learning About God Through the Bible

Objectives

God reveals himself through Scripture in a variety of ways. In this session, parents will

- talk about some historical and cultural misperceptions about God.
- discuss different types of communication found in the Bible and how they each help us understand God.
- explore different ways the Bible helps us know God.

Notes and Tips

1. Remember the importance of starting and ending on time.

2. As an example to the group, it is important that you and your spouse complete the HomeBuilders Project each session.

3. During Wrap-Up, make a point to encourage couples to "Make a Date" to complete the HomeBuilders Project for this session.

4. You may find it helpful to make some notes right after the meeting to help you evaluate how this session went. Ask yourself questions such as "Did everyone participate? Is there anyone I need to make a special effort to follow up with before the next session?"

Commentary

Note: The numbers that follow correspond to the Blueprints questions of the same numbers in the session.

2. The total contents of the Bible are beyond human invention. They are literally the words from God's

LEADER NOTES **135**

heart and mind. The writers did not write what they wanted to say but what God communicated to them as his revelation.

4. The Gospels can offer insight into the way God relates to people. The letters of Paul and others allow us to understand how people who knew Jesus related to him and interpreted his life and teachings. Books like Psalms and Proverbs allow us to gain a sense of how a person who did not see Jesus related to and understood God. The book of Acts lets us see the results of the living God and Jesus working in the lives of people.

9. A few ideas on how you can help make Bible stories come alive include: acting out stories as a family, reading to your children from Bible storybooks that edit the stories into contemporary language, and purchasing or checking out videos of Bible stories.

| Leader Notes |

Session Four:
Learning About God Through His Attributes

Objectives

Knowing the attributes of God can help give your children a vision of the true God.

In this session parents will

- study how God reveals his character through different descriptions of himself in the Bible.
- look at Jesus as the bread of life.
- consider how they can help their children better know God by teaching them about God's titles and attributes.

Notes and Tips

1. By this time, group members should be getting more comfortable with each other. For prayer at the end of this session, you may want to give everyone an opportunity to pray by asking the group to finish a sentence that goes something like this: "Lord, I want to thank you for..." Be sensitive to anyone who may not feel comfortable doing this.

2. Congratulations! You are halfway through this study. It's time for a checkup: How's the group going? What has worked well so far? What things might you consider changing as you approach this and the remaining sessions?

3. You and your spouse may want to consider writing notes of thanks and encouragement to the members of your group this week. Thank them for their commitment and contribution to the group, and let them know that you're praying for them. (Make a point to pray from them as you write their notes.)

LEADER NOTES **137**

Commentary

Note: The numbers that follow correspond to the Blueprints questions of the same numbers in the session.

3. God is personal and has a personal name. He is the one who revealed himself to Abraham, Isaac, and Jacob. And God is the same as he was when he met with Abraham, Isaac, and Jacob. God is the same from generation to generation.

5. As the Lamb of God (John 1:29), Jesus can help us learn to be gentle and meek in dealing with others.

As the good shepherd (John 10:11), Jesus can help us learn to take care of others.

As the Lion of the tribe of Judah (Revelation 5:5), Jesus can be seen protecting those who are helpless or defending God's character.

10. Jesus was using hyperbole to tell the people that bread would not completely satisfy their deepest needs that are spiritual. Bread provides protein, complex carbohydrates, vitamins, iron, fiber, and other nutrients we need for living. But life is more than the physical—Jesus is the "bread" that can satisfy our heart and soul.

11. Deuteronomy 8:3 highlights the very thing Jesus was saying. Physical food is not enough to satisfy all the needs of each individual human being. The very words of God are the most satisfying resources we have to find fulfillment.

---| **Leader Notes** |---

Session Five:
Learning About God Through Jesus Christ

Objectives

To really know God, you and your children must know Jesus Christ.

In this session parents will

- look at who Jesus is.
- explore different ways the words and actions of Jesus reflect God's character.
- discuss ways to use the life of Christ to teach their children about God.

Notes and Tips

1. Looking ahead: For the next session—the last one of this course—you may want to ask a person or a couple to share what this course or group has meant to him or her. (You can ask them to share during the Warm-Up or Wrap-Up time.) Be thinking and praying about this.

Commentary

1. John 1:1-5, 14 tells us that Jesus, the Word, has always been with God and that he came to reveal the Father to the world. Note: In the original Greek language, the phrase in John 1:14 that reads that Jesus "made his dwelling among us" means "he pitched his tent" among us.

Note: The numbers that follow correspond to the Blueprints questions of the same numbers in the session.

LEADER NOTES **139**

John 14:5-11 says Jesus and God the Father are one and the same.

Colossians 1:15 tells us Christ is the perfect image of God, whom we cannot see.

2. This question is designed to force group members to think about what they know of Jesus. If the group has trouble answering the question, turn to passages that illustrate both Jesus' divine and human natures. For example, to illustrate the divine, see Matthew 8:26-27 (Jesus calms a storm), Matthew 14:19-21 (the feeding of the five thousand), Mark 2:8 (Jesus displays the ability to know what men are thinking), and John 2:1-11 (Jesus turns water into wine).

To illustrate Christ's humanity, acknowledge, if not already identified by the group, that Jesus had needs and emotions common to us all: He ate, slept, wept, got angry, and was at times weary, thirsty, and sad. Matthew 26:37-39 reveals the personal, human emotions that Jesus faced.

3. Jesus was interested in people on a very personal level. Jesus loves us and shows us compassion, in spite of our sin and faults.

5. A few examples of Christlike compassion you might share if they do not come up in the group discussion: Standing up for others who are being left out or mistreated. Spending time with children or adults who do not receive much attention, don't have many friends, or have special needs.

6. There was already a market where all these things could be done. The merchants were taking advantage of the need for sacrificial animals probably with the approval of the Temple elders. God's meeting place for fellowship with his people was being misused and abused.

7. God's anger is fierce like a burning fire. It is directed at those who do not serve or recognize him as creator and worthy of worship.

8. It may be interesting to note that sometimes we get angry about the very weaknesses in others that we have and for which we are not willing to change or submit to God.

10. Christ maintained his divine nature and purpose. Jesus was willing to grant forgiveness to the repentant thief and let judgment rest on the one that would not believe.

| Leader Notes |

Session Six:
Responding to God

Objectives

God takes the initiative in pursuing a relationship with our children and us, but a response is also called for.

In this session parents will

- study how God pursues a relationship with us.
- examine four responses to God: love, fear, trust, and obedience.
- discuss practical ways to encourage our children to respond to God.

Notes and Tips

1. While this HomeBuilders study has great value, people are likely to return to previous patterns of living unless they commit to a plan for carrying on the progress that they've made. During this final session of the course, encourage couples to take specific steps beyond this series to continue to build God-honoring homes. For example, you may want to challenge couples who have developed the habit of a date night during the course of this study to continue this practice. Also, you may want the group to consider doing another HomeBuilders study.

2. For Extra Impact: Here's a suggestion for making the closing prayer time for this last session special. Have the group form a prayer circle. Then have each person or couple, if comfortable doing so, take a turn standing or kneeling in the middle of the circle while the group prays specifically for them.

142   HELPING YOUR CHILDREN KNOW GOD

3. As a part of this last session, devote time for planning one more meeting—a party to celebrate the completion of this study!

Commentary

3. We should delight in a relationship with God more than any other relationship we have. We should strive to put God's will, desires, and purposes first in our lives each day.

Note: The numbers that follow correspond to the Blueprints questions of the same numbers in the session.

4. In our popular culture, love seems to be portrayed as primarily self-centered and is frequently characterized in these ways:

- I love you because you love me.
- I love you because of what you can do for me.
- I love you because of what I get from you or what I can get because of you.

However, our love for God should be, in one sense, a consuming passion. It should also be based on respect and gratefulness. We respect God because God is holy and perfect, and yet he wants to fellowship with us. We are grateful to God because God provides salvation and daily provision for us, never leaves us, is always faithful to us, and his love and provision are free to us through Christ Jesus.

5. Adam and Eve feared God because they had disobeyed and did not know how God would react or what the outcome would be. The fear of the Lord in Psalm 34 is awe—respect of God's holiness and power.

8. We need to put our trust in God not only when facing crises, major decisions, dealing with our sin, and when we have specific needs, but also practically, on a day-to-day basis. Trusting God daily helps us be better able to stand in faith against the trials of life.

LEADER NOTES

Does Your Church Offer Marriage Insurance?

Great marriages don't just happen—husbands and wives need to nurture them. They need to make their marriage relationship a priority.

That's where the HomeBuilders Couples Series® can help! The series consists of interactive 6- to 7-week small group studies that make it easy couples to really open up with each other. The result is fun, non-threaten interactions that build stronger Christ-centered relationships between spouses—and with other couples!

Whether you've been married for years or are newly married, this seri will help you and your spouse discover timeless principles from God's Wo that you can apply to your marriage and make it the best it can be!

The HomeBuilders Leader Guide gives you all the information and encouragement you need to start and lead a dynamic HomeBuilders small group.

The HomeBuilders Couples Series includes these life-changing studies:
- Building Teamwork in Your Marriage
- Building Your Marriage *(also available in Spanish!)*
- Building Your Mate's Self-Esteem
- Growing Together in Christ
- Improving Communication in Your Marriage *(also available in Spanish!)*
- Making Your Remarriage Last
- Mastering Money in Your Marriage
- Overcoming Stress in Your Marriage
- Resolving Conflict in Your Marriage

And check out the HomeBuilders Parenting Series!
- Building Character in Your Children
- Establishing Effective Discipline for Your Children
- Guiding Your Teenagers
- Helping Your Children Know (
- Improving Your Parenting
- Raising Children of Faith

Look for the **HomeBuilders Couples Ser** and **HomeBuilders Parenting Series** at your favorite Christian supplier or write:

www.familylife.com

P.O. Box 485, Loveland, CO 80539-04
www.grouppublishing.com